LEARNING
IN TANDEM

involving parents
in their children's education

RU   ND

© 1996 Ruth Merttens, Alan Newland and Susie Webb

Published by Scholastic Ltd
Villiers House
Clarendon Avenue
Leamington Spa
Warwickshire CV32 5PR

Authors Ruth Merttens, Alan Newland and Susie Webb
Editors Noel Pritchard and Joel Lane
Assistant Editor Libby Weaver
Series Designer Lynne Joesbury
Designer Claire Belcher

Designed using Aldus Pagemaker
Printed in Great Britain by Bell & Bain Ltd, Glasgow

The right of Ruth Merttens, Alan Newland and Susie Webb to be
identified as the Authors of this Work has been asserted by them
in accordance with the Copyright, Designs and Patents Act 1988

British Library Cataloguing-in-Publication Data
A catalogue record for this book is available from the British Library.

ISBN 0-590-53428-9

© Material from the National Curriculum is Crown copyright and
is reproduced by permission of the Controller of HMSO, 1995.

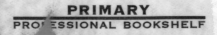

PRIMARY
PROFESSIONAL BOOKSHELF

CONTENTS

PRIMARY
PROFESSIONAL BOOKSHELF

FOREWORD

There is something truly bizarre about the idea of schools as institutions operating entirely separately from parents. As a parent, I have sometimes thought that what we do is bring our children to school in the morning and throw them over the wall. Then in the evening, the teachers throw them back to us. There's a history to the division of labour between parents and teachers. In the state school system, there has long been a pervasive feeling that schools are essentially civilising places which compensate for middle-class parents mollycoddling their children and for working-class parents neglecting and brutalising theirs. Schools would (and should) knock the edges off the spoilt kids, lick the wayward ones into shape, introduce children to the timetables and work schedules of 'real life' and shine a little light into the lives of the backward and benighted. It has been possible to characterise schools as having a culture of their own, with stated and unwritten rules, an ethos and a tone. With a few moments' thought, we can all conjure up pictures of how, when we were at school, we were, say, grouped in class or lined up in the playground (or not), how assemblies were run or how official days like Nativity Plays, Sports Days or Prize Days were organised. It is through these practices that schools define what kind of place they are, and what their attitudes towards children and parents are. Part of this process of definition will always entail creating explicit and implicit messages about what kind of culture is acceptable and what is not. All of us, as ex-pupils or teachers, can remember hearing phrases like 'that kind of behaviour is just not acceptable here'.

But whereas we might all be agreed that it's not OK for children to break windows or tear up other children's work, the phrase has also been used in much more contentious contexts. The recollections of many disabled children in the 1930s, working-class children in grammar schools in the 1950s, or black children in the 1960s testify to the experience of being treated by schools as outsiders. Such children felt themselves to be marked as undesirables unless certain crucial cultural and behavioural changes were made: accents dropped, deference procedures taken up, and so on. In a broader perspective, several sociological critiques draw attention to the ways in which schools may be said to pass on the dominant culture of the day – and, more subtly, to favour those children who come from homes that are part of that dominant culture.

The argument as to whether this is so has been at the heart of the last twenty years' worth of educational discussion and legislation in most Western countries. At various times and on different occasions, the word 'parents' has been flung into the fray. Politicians and popular newspapers, largely in favour of testing the 'knowledge' transmitted by means of formal tests or exams, have claimed to have parents on their side. 'What the parents want...' has been a useful preface to many of their statements. Parent governors (an idea first introduced systematically by the now-abolished ILEA) were meant to be an additional arm to support the government's policies. Yet in many parts of the country, particularly in Scotland, parents co-operated with teachers to prevent the implementation of government tests, and have continued this co-operation in forming a united opposition to government cuts in education spending.

But there has been something rather unthought-out about all this invoking and mobilising of parents. What *should* the role of parents in education be? Successive ministers have identified this as 'turning off the television' or 'teaching children the difference between right and wrong'; while some teachers have, rather defensively, insisted that they as professionals should decide what should be taught and how.

This book is particularly welcome because its premise is that parents are natural and inevitable partners in education. If, in a school, either teachers or parents feel antagonistic towards the other party, then you can be sure that children will not feel like learning very much or very effectively within the formal curriculum. I said 'either teachers or parents'! With a little thought we can all think of situations in which one or the other group has been up in arms: 'The parents round here don't care about their kids' education...' or 'The teachers are all rubbish, they don't teach the kids how to spell any more...', and so on. This book faces up to the fact that we can only progress in education if some real co-operation goes on between parents and teachers. It shows how this cannot be simply haphazard or informal – which inevitably involves cliques and disillusionment – but has to have agendas and organisation to make it work. It provides a review of the relevant arguments, theories and research, and makes a set of pragmatic suggestions for implementing an effective partnership.

It seems to me that a situation in which parents, children, schools and teachers perceive themselves as competing with one another, either for the best 'results' or for the 'best' children, or indeed for the best resources, is a massively wasteful and socially disastrous way of going on. For fair teacher-parent co-operation to take place, it needs to take place in a wider context than just one school or one area. This book is a step along the way.

Michael Rosen
October, 1995

INTRODUCTION
AND OVERVIEW

Conversation at about 4.00 pm, anywhere in the country....
Parent: 'What did you do at school today?'
Child: 'Nothing.'

As the director of IMPACT, the largest project on parental involvement in Britain, I address on average one parent meeting per week in different schools located all over the country. I always ask parents what their children answer to the question posed above. Their response is guaranteed to be the same – 'Nothing!' Speaking as a parent of six children myself, I can sympathise. If I press my nine-year-old hard, he may grudgingly release a small nugget of information. 'I had pink custard for lunch,' or 'I had a fight with Robert in the playground.' I get no news whatever about his academic achievements – or lack of the same! Contrast this with my youngest child Matthew's statement when he came home after his third day at school – 'It was real good at school today. Mrs Clark put Thomas on the "T" table!'

Almost all primary schools, and a majority of secondary schools, have a policy nowadays which states that they involve parents in the life and work of the school. The evidence is strong that parents actually do want to be involved and are interested in what is going on. Martin Hughes reported that an overwhelming majority of parents were interested in their child's progress in the primary phase[1]; and the work of Ron Glatter, Phil Woods and others at the Open University[2] suggests that the same is true for parents of children entering the secondary phase. All the research we have done on IMPACT[3] points in the same direction – parents are overwhelmingly interested in what their children are doing at school and how they are getting on. If asked, parents commonly report that they would like more information than they currently receive – either via the official school processes or via their child.

However, it is worth analysing the precise nature of the parents' interest. Most parents are predominantly interested in their own child's progress and those aspects of school life which specifically relate to him or her. They are not necessarily interested in the curriculum, the management of the school, the state of the school finances, the number of school trips and so on, except in so far as any one of these relates directly and immediately to their child at that time. This explains why 90 per cent of parents will show up at the beginning or end of the year to see their child's teacher for the personal interview, while less than 20 per cent may turn out to the annual governor's meeting or a curriculum evening. This is not to say that parents on the whole are not interested in the collective well-being of the whole school. However, it does emphasise the fact that it is primarily and predominantly those things most directly connected to their child's progress and welfare which are top of their agenda.

We would have to agree that this is reasonable enough. As one education officer said to me recently, 'I probably wouldn't be interested in attending annual governors' meetings if I didn't have to!' And usually, parents are not professionally interested in education. The mysteries of the third version of the National Curriculum in maths, or the finer details of the DFE draft circular on school attendance figures, are not matters which are necessarily of absorbing interest to the average parent. However, the fact that Matthew's teacher is leaving next term and that the school may not be able to replace her will focus a great deal of my concern and that of the other parents in his class.

Parental involvement in the curriculum reaches to the heart of the specific and particular nature of parents' concerns. The ways in which parents can come to be involved are numerous and will depend upon a variety of factors, including the age of the child, the curriculum subject and the situation of the school. This book will encompass a large number of different methods which teachers and schools across the UK and in the United States have utilised to involve parents directly in their children's learning. The book will also draw upon the available research, and current theoretical work, in order to present its case. We have divided up the field of parental involvement in the curriculum, breaking it down to consider the particular issues associated with different subjects and age ranges of children. However, each chapter follows roughly the same format:

✦ An overview of the theoretical background to, and the recent research findings in, the particular area under discussion.

✦ A discussion of the implications of the research into, and theories behind, parental participation in schools and playgroups.

✦ An outline of pragmatic and practical suggestions for ways of involving parents in this area.

Each chapter utilises a system of sub-sections labelled with clear headings for ease of access. Some of the theoretical writing and research which we draw upon is complex and, on occasion, involves difficult ideas or structures. We have tried to present these in a clear way, without resorting to an oversimplification which does not do justice to the complexity or subtlety of the ideas referred to. The headings provide a means by which the reader can keep track of the arguments or analyses being described.

Chapter 1 concerns the early years of children's lives, and focuses upon the development of language and the implications of both recent research and current theory for our practice in schools, nursery classes and playgroups. Chapters 2, 3 and 4 discuss parental participation in (respectively) children's learning to read, their learning of maths and their learning to write. In each case, the first section provides a theoretical framework for the subsequent discussion. Chapter 5 considers the wider curriculum, and the issues involved in collaborating with parents and with utilising and drawing upon both the expertise of the parents and the culture of the communities in which the children live. The conclusion to the book draws the various threads together, in terms both of theoretical ideas and of pragmatic suggestions. The argument for parental involvement in the curriculum is grounded in a discussion of the different pedagogies at home and in school, exemplified by means of research data drawn from the authors' own experiences.

In this introduction, I aim to provide an overview of the field of parental involvement in the curriculum. The various ways in which parents can be, or have been, involved in partnership projects or collaborative schemes are described and categorised under generic headings. However, before commencing on this outline it is useful to establish a shared model for the processes involved in educating children in the setting of the classroom. We have drawn up the following diagram to elaborate this model:

TEACH

✦ Teachers actively instruct, narrate, model and explain.

MAKE SENSE

✦ Children make this knowledge their own, and make sense of what they have been taught through a variety of means, including stories, practical activities, problem-solving tasks, games, puzzles and investigative, exploratory and creative work.

PRACTISE

✦ Skills often require practice and reinforcement. This can be achieved through activities on an individual basis, in pairs and in small groups.

This model of classroom practice places teaching at the heart of the process. Teaching does not necessarily imply a whole-class lesson, nor does it refer to a didactic chalk-and-talk session. Teaching on this model is an *active* process, which may involve a number of ways of operating:

✦ *Modelling* – The teacher models how to write, or read, or to do a particular piece of maths. This is important because the teacher models many activities, from writing a poem to building a circuit, some of which the children might never see outside the context of the classroom.

✦ *Instructing* – In order to make procedures explicit, including those that the children may design themselves, the teacher frequently gives a series of instructions: 'Hold the number in your head, and count on...', 'Put your finger on the line to leave a space between words...'

✦ *Narrating* – Stories are a major means by which teachers can help children to see a point or become interested in a topic. Even in maths, children often need a context in order to make sense of a particular process. As Martin Hughes points out in *Children and Number*, there is a wealth of difference between the question 'What's three and one more?' and the question 'What's three giraffes and one more?' Given a narrative-context, many children can do things they cannot do in a more abstract or disembedded way.

✦ *Directing attention* – Teachers direct children's attention to many things: to specific facts, to ways of doing things, to stories, poems, works of art and scientific processes, to name but a few. We use explanation as a means of creating and sustaining the joint attention of the children, and ourselves on the subject being taught.

Once children have been taught something, they need to make sense of it for themselves; otherwise there was no point in their having been taught it in the first place. The means by which children make sense of things varies according to what is being studied and the age of the children. Traditionally, practical activities have been used to help young children understand what they are doing. Stories also play a crucial role in the process of making sense, as we shall see in chapters 1 and 2. In addition, teachers utilise a variety of different strategies and activities such as games, puzzles and exploratory or investigative tasks. What all these have in common is that they all require *talk*. In order to make sense of things, children need to talk them through. Speech has, as we shall see in Chapter 4, a regulatory function in helping children learn. So it is crucial that the process of classroom education allows for the role of talk, and facilitates this aspect of learning.

Many skills require some practice, and some skills require a great deal. It is possible to over-practise a skill, and children can actually get worse rather than better! However, some practice is essential if certain skills are to become 'automatic'. Thus the transcriptional aspects of writing and the number bond aspects of addition or multiplication both need to be automatic skills by the time children reach the age of ten or eleven. This means that they will have had to practise these skills many times over a number of years. The context in which this practice occurs can and should be varied, and does not need to be boring or even repetitive. Children can be writing interesting and creative works of literature or applying their mathematical skills in order to solve a science problem.

The model described above allows us to identify both the teachers' and the parents' role. For example, homework, in its traditional form, has usually involved some type of routine practice. However, some of the shared homework schemes described in chapters 3 and 4 locate the home-tasks firmly within the 'making sense' category. They are predicated upon the notion that the one thing all children can do better and more effectively at home than at school is talk. And talk is the major factor needed to help children make sense of something. Thus we shall utilise this model as we consider, in each chapter, where the role of parents in the home and that of teachers in the classroom can interconnect.

AN OVERVIEW OF PARENTAL INVOLVEMENT IN THE CURRICULUM

The rest of this introductory chapter will be concerned with categorising and describing the various ways in which schools, nursery classes and playgroups can involve parents in the curriculum. These will be discussed in general terms, under the appropriate headings.

PARENTS IN THE CLASSROOM

Many schools invite parents to assist teachers in the classroom. In more than one area in the country, a project has been set up in connection with the Open College Network whereby parents who work alongside teachers in this way can, in collaboration with a college tutor, provide a specified programme of activities for the children and evaluate its effectiveness. This will then lead to the award of a qualification, the level of the qualification depending on the level of the work prepared by the parent.

A particular issue in this context concerns the questions which arise about parents working in the same classrooms as their own children. As usual, practices differ – some teachers prefer to keep parents in different classrooms from their own children, while others find that it works best when they are together. There has been some research into this question in relation to parents reading with children, and in chapter 2 these questions will be fully discussed.

The various ways in which teachers and parents can work together in classrooms will be explored in relation to the different subject areas. Many parents do not feel confident about offering to help children with maths, although they are quite happy to read with children or to engage in an art activity. Many more parents are to be found in nursery and infant classrooms than in the juniors'. Clearly, one factor here is the fact that parents are often more likely to return to work as their children grow older. However, feelings of increased insecurity and lack of confidence with the work which older children are expected to do in class also play a part. There are established ways in which teachers can help to reassure parents and to encourage those who are keen to continue their role in classroom work. These are also outlined in chapters 2 and 3.

LEARNING ACTIVITIES IN THE HOME

Many parents – probably most parents – help their children with maths and writing, or with reading at home. All parents are, in a real sense, their children's first educators in that they provide the rich linguistic environment in which children learn to speak. It is also the case that many home activities, routinely performed in the course of family life, have an important function in helping to develop a particular skill or increase the child's knowledge about a specific topic. The IMPACT project, as well as others, has carried out extensive research into the nature and quality of the learning which occurs naturally (that is to say, unprompted by the school) in the home. Throughout this book we will refer to, and comment upon, these findings, contextualising them by providing suggestions for ways in which teachers can support and encourage children's learning in the home.

Some parts of this book concern themselves with the question of the invisibility and visibility of pedagogic practices in relation to children's acquisition of mathematical or literacy skills. A teacher may recognise that sorting the washing can be a highly productive context for rehearsing various mathematical skills – sorting, counting, classifying, and so on. Once a parent has been alerted to this fact, they may sometimes approach this task with its pedagogic as well as its practical functions in mind. This notion that school-designed activities may, if taken home and shared, render other aspects of home-focused tasks (like laying the table or sorting the washing) visible as 'classroom maths' is one which we shall explore at some length in the final chapter.

CURRICULUM EVENINGS AND PARENT/TEACHER WORKING PARTIES

Teachers can encourage parental participation by including them in the planning of curriculum evenings and also, less commonly, in discussions about curriculum policy. Talking to a group of parents about the approaches taken to the teaching of writing or of maths, the ways in which scientific ideas are introduced to children and the technology curriculum is an excellent way of bridging the gap between what parents sometimes expect, based on vague memories of their own schooling, and current educational thinking. Any documentation or information produced may then be said genuinely to be a 'whole-school policy'. We shall discuss throughout the book the innovative practices which have been developed by some schools keen to involve parents in this area of school management and policy.

SHARED HOMEWORK SCHEMES

The strong interest of parents in their own children's learning is one of the reasons why so many of the shared reading, and shared maths, homework schemes have been successful. Through helping the child – or being helped by the child – with a task which is part of the routine classwork for that week, the parent gains in several ways:

✦ They see the child working and get an idea of the sorts of things that the child is doing in class.

✦ The child actually talks about his work – often having to explain the finer points to his parent.

✦ The parent can observe the child reading, doing maths or writing for himself in the context of the home, and can therefore contribute valuable information to any discussion with the teacher about the child.

✦ This experience will be the basis for a more informed dialogue with the teacher about curriculum matters.

Part of each chapter will be devoted to structured systems of collaborative homework tasks. Using 'homework' (work done at home) in this way, as a vehicle for parental participation, provides one of the most effective means of involving all parents in their own children's learning. There is ample evidence[4] that parents can, and will, help children through sharing activities and tasks which the teacher selects and sends for the children to do at home. The results of these tasks then feed back into the classroom curriculum.

This practice of sending activities to be shared in the home is a far cry from that of traditional homework. The differences can be summarised as follows:

✦ Traditional homework takes no account of the *situation* – it consists of practice activities, pieces of writing, pages of sums, and so on, which could be done in the classroom or could be done in the home. They pay no attention to the home context.

✦ Homework was supposed to be done *alone and unaided*. Although many children did in fact get help from their parents or from older siblings, this was never encouraged and mostly remained hidden.

✦ Homework, as traditionally conceived, can be socially divisive. What happens if the child or pupil is stuck and unable to do the sums or complete the task? Those parents who possess the requisite knowledge and competencies are able to assist and take the role of the 'teacher in the home'. Those parents who 'failed' at school are now in a situation where they feel themselves to be failing a second time. They find themselves unable to help, and this may well cause distress to both children and parents. This distress is worsened by the fact that the children are aware that some children's parents do possess the skills to offer help at these points. Thus the inequalities are perpetuated.

The programmes of shared activity outlined in this book avoid the disadvantages of traditional homework and, at the same time, open up a dialogue between home and school. The activities could include a book to read, a mathematical game or a piece of writing. Each chapter has a different focus, and where reading, writing, maths or the other curriculum areas are discussed, suitable tasks or activities will be presented as examples.

THE HISTORY OF PARENTAL INVOLVEMENT IN THE CURRICULUM

The last ten years have witnessed an extraordinary growth in both the quantity and the scope of schemes to encourage this type of collaboration by parents in their children's learning. It is worth considering three factors which have all been influential in encouraging these developments.

1. A change in the role of the professional
In the 1980s there was an increasing shift in the relationship between the 'professional' and the 'laity'. Fifty years earlier, George Bernard Shaw had reminded us that 'all professions are conspiracies against the laity', but it took a long while before attitudes were to soften sufficiently to enable a real change to take place. Patients visiting their doctors became more likely to expect a discussion about possible forms of treatment. Women having babies expressed a real, and in some cases a violent, dissatisfaction with a mode of treatment in which they became the passive recipients of the 'expert's advice'. They demanded – and got – a say in the ways they were to be prepared for the birth, the types and amount of medication they were to receive and the mode of delivery. Mothers checking into baby clinics expected a real dialogue to take place between the health visitor – whose expertise lay in seeing many hundreds of babies during the course of their work – and the mother herself – whose 'expert knowledge' resided in her familiarity with all the specificities and peculiarities of this one baby.

The changes here amounted to a seismic shift in the very foundations of the relationship between professional and 'client', and schools and teachers were not immune from the effects of this. Parents started to become more of a force to be reckoned with. They could no longer be guaranteed to back up the teacher under all circumstances, and increasingly looked to be supplied with information and choices in situations where once the teacher's decision was a purely private matter. If the circumstances became extreme or severe enough, communication between parents and teachers could break down completely, as was the case in the William Tyndale affair. As part of his justification for how the school had behaved, the Headteacher gave an interesting analogy. He described teachers as being like electricians, and pointed out that only a fool invites an electrician to wire his house and then tells him how to do it. In making this comparison, he drew heavily upon a notion of a professional and restricted expertise, and an implicit and complete trust on the part of the recipient. However, as history demonstrates, his faith in this relationship was misplaced. Parents could no longer see themselves as passive clients in this sense, nor were they prepared to leave something as precious as the education of their children entirely to the 'experts'.

This is not to deny the importance and crucial nature of teachers' expertise. It is simply to emphasise that parents − like patients and pregnant women − are no longer content to be a silent, and passively accepting, majority. Most take it for granted that they will play an active role in supporting what is done in school as well as in monitoring their children's progress.

2. Parental involvement in reading

In the late 1970s and early '80s, there were several projects which were influential in terms of demonstrating the importance of the parents' role in supporting children's learning to read. These projects included The Haringey Project, the Pitfield Project, the Coventry Project and the Belfield Reading Project, although there were many others as well, such as those in Dagenham and Reading.[5] Put simply, the results of these projects were such as to make everyone in education sit up and take notice. It was clear that a sustained and committed programme of encouraging regular parental assistance with children's reading paid good dividends, not only in terms of scores on reading tests, but also in terms of children's attitudes and motivation.

Since the publication of these results, schools, particularly those in the nursery and infant sector, have actively encouraged parents to read and share books with their children at home. Indeed, this now sounds such an obvious policy of 'good common sense' that it is difficult to imagine schools doing otherwise. But, as I usually point out to trainee-teachers, in educational terms this has been a particularly rapid and thoroughgoing change in approach. When I took my first son (who is now 22!) to primary school, quite the opposite view was the norm. On his first day the teacher, explaining what she thought we ought to know as 'new' parents, said that she did hope that we would, none of us, read with our children at home, as they did find that it confused the children so. We all promised that we would not dream of doing anything so dangerous. Of course, I expect that all of us did continue to read – secretly and with a not-quite clean conscience – with our children, notwithstanding the advice!

The majority of schools, even those that do not utilise any other form of homework, do send a reading book home with each child, and ask that this should be shared by an adult or older sibling. There are a wide variety of ways in which this 'shared reading' can be organised, and we shall be discussing the advantages and disadvantages of the different methods in chapters 1 and 2. It is certainly the case that the prevalence, scope and variety of these practices is impressive and indicates the consensus which now exists as to the crucial nature of the parent's role.

3. The use of homework as a vehicle for parental participation

There has not been a tradition of homework in English primary schools since the '60s. Many teachers were trained at a time when it was argued that homework belonged to an era of didactic 'chalk and talk' and the wielding of the cane, and had no place in a more progressive and child-centred education system. Alongside many other reforms of that period, the coherence of this view is now being questioned. Parents wish to help their children. Teachers have to ensure that children acquire a large number of important and 'basic' skills upon which they will now be tested at the end of each key stage. Some of these skills require a fair element of practice and this practice

needs to occur in a variety of different contexts. Thus children need to practise number skills in the context of games, puzzles and 'real-life' problems as well as doing sums in a maths book. They need to be able to write both imaginatively and factually, and to understand the different styles appropriate to different genres. The home offers a rich source of out-of-school contexts, and parents can provide much-needed individual support.

Recent school inspections, including HMI, have certainly perceived the parental aspect of homework as crucial. The OFSTED inspection schedule refers to homework, as does the questionnaire sent by the inspectors to parents. All this reflects current official thinking, which now sees homework in the primary school as a sign of good practice. The nature and type of this homework, its purpose and the forms it should take are currently being debated at all levels of education. This book informs this debate, and suggests persuasive practical and theoretical reasons why homework might be viewed as a form of parental participation rather than as a 'back-to-basics' strategy.

PARENTS AND TEACHERS TOGETHER

The idea that as teachers we *need* parents, that parents are not 'an optional extra', not just the icing on the cake but a crucial part of the mixture itself, is not new. But it does sometimes require a little emphasis to ensure that the implications for both whole-school approach and resourcing are really taken on board. As far back as 1985, the Norman Thomas Report recognised the vital contributions of parents in assisting children's learning to read, and highly commended the work of projects such as PACT (Parents and Children and Teachers, Hackney, 1984). They recommended 'that a scheme be set up and monitored whereby parents are involved in their children's learning of maths in the same way as they have been for reading.'[6] These remarks heralded the birth of the IMPACT Project.

In addition to these powerful and persuasive arguments, we have the undeniable and regrettable fact that class sizes are rising. As a consequence, trying to give every one of 35 or 40 children the personal and highly-sensitive and contingent support they require becomes even less possible. In common with many infant teachers,

I like to stress to parents the crucial nature of the part they play. 'If all the reading your child does is the reading she does while she is actually in this classroom, it is going to take her a very long time to learn to read,' I warn them, 'because, with the best will in the world, I cannot listen sufficiently to each child each week to enable them to make satisfactory progress in learning to read. Children need to read often, ideally every day – not for long, but a little each day. Only in this way can we guarantee that they will achieve what they are capable of.' And the parents overwhelmingly do respond by co-operating. They usually don't read every day at home with their child, but they *do* read two or three times a week. Some parents also come into school and sit and read with the children. Some assist by running after-school reading clubs or book fairs. And all of this helps.

PARENTS BUYING 'WORK' BOOKS

Sales of 'outside school' textbooks – purchased by parents off the shelf at high street bookshops – have blossomed. A myth circulates among teachers that it is only the so-called 'pushy' parents who buy these. However, this is contradicted by the evidence, since these books sell in their millions. It is a fact that working-class parents buy just as many as their middle-class counterparts. And in their purchase of these books, parents from all walks of life demonstrate that they are willing and able to support their children's learning.

Schools in general, and primary specialists in particular, have disapproved of both the sale and purchase of these books – without, of course, being able to prevent their production. It is interesting to consider the reasons in which this disapproval is rooted. Many of the books adopt a more traditional style and pedagogy than current primary teachers feel comfortable with. Maths books are characterised by neat rows of sums, language books by spellings and phonics. Many use stereotypical images – teachers in mortarboards, with blackboards and easels. However, these factors also apply to at least some of the books to be found in most school libraries, and do not, in themselves, account for the strength of disapproval.

In order to see what it is about these books that disturbs us as teachers, we have to probe a little deeper than their 'old-fashioned' style. The books rely heavily on practice – they provide paper and pencil contexts for practising the so-called 'basic' skills. Teachers may, with reason, feel that the prevalence of this type of book encourages a tendency for parents to value only this type of paper-and-pencil activity and to devalue the more active or context-based activities often on view in the classroom. They may also wonder whether children who have been bribed or coerced into spending their time doing pages of sums or writing practice at home may not prove such enthusiastic learners in the classroom.

However, against these objections, it may be countered that some children actually do enjoy these books – arguably the majority of those who do them. There is certainly a satisfaction to be obtained from completing a set of sums or several lines of 'copying'. Some children like the sensation of 'playing at school'; and often the tasks provided within these books are not intellectually demanding or challenging, requiring little more than procedural knowledge or memory skills and patience. Success in correctly completing a page is therefore not hard to achieve.

The question is, do these books actually do any harm? Should we, as teachers, be discouraging their use? At present, many parents will actually hide the fact that they buy and use these books at home from the teacher, just as they will conceal the fact that they also buy certain reading schemes. After nearly ten years of talking to many hundreds of parents about this through the research programme attached to the IMPACT project, we take the following line. If schools offer a sufficiency of school-based activities for children and parents to share at home, much of the rationale behind the parental purchase of these books will vanish. Furthermore, the provision of regular and shared home activities by the school will greatly enhance the parents' understanding of the nature, and type, of the activities and tasks which teachers regard as appropriate for each stage in each subject. Thus the type of programme described in each of the following chapters goes a long way toward solving the problem. And, in cases where parents still prefer to augment the educational diet of their child with these books, it must be a good thing to allow for this to be the subject of an open and friendly discussion between teacher and parent rather than leaving it as unspoken. Again, the parental participation programmes described throughout this book set up and sustain mechanisms which facilitate precisely this type of discussion.

COMBATING DISADVANTAGE

Parental involvement in the curriculum is particularly important since it provides a direct input into what children are actually doing at school. We know that at all levels, the parents' sustained interest in what is happening to the child at school is likely to be a crucial factor in future educational success. It is important to be clear about what is at stake here. The research evidence is unequivocal in demonstrating that, however we categorise it, the socio-economic background of the home is the biggest single factor in predicting children's educational attainment.[7] However, further research also proves that parents can, and do, make a difference.[8] And behind all this, there is some, although more equivocal, evidence that teachers and schools also make a difference!

Given that this is the somewhat depressing backdrop against which we have to work, it seems foolish not to recognise the crucial nature of collaboration with parents. Professor Peter Coleman, working with Joan Collinge in Canada has suggested that it is 'learning triads' – i.e. the parent, child and teacher – which may be considered the unit of educational effectiveness. And in England, John Bastiani[9] has stressed that, although it does not always make life simple, it is essential to build on good practice in working together since the results of not doing so can be dire. The question, then, that schools in general and teachers in particular need to ask is no longer *whether* to involve parents in their children's learning, but *how*.

Ruth Merttens

REFERENCES

1 Hughes, M., Wikeley, F. and Nash, T. (1994) *Parents and Their Children's Schools*, Basil Blackwell.

2 Glatter, R. and Woods, P. (1992) 'Parental Choice and School Decision-Making: Operating in a Market-like Environment', Commonwealth Council for Educational Administration, University of Hong Kong.

3 Merttens, R. and Vass, J. (1992) *Sharing Maths Cultures* Falmer Press.

Merttens, R. and Vass, J. (1993) *Partnerships in Maths: Parents and Schools* Falmer Press.

Merttens, R. and Woods, P. (1994) 'IMPACT at AERA', University of North London Press.

'The IMPACT Project in Haringey: Raising Standards in Inner City Schools' (1994). A report to the DFE.

4 Topping, K. and Wolfendale, S. (1985) *Parental Involvement in Children's Reading*, Croom Helm, London.

Hamilton, D. and Griffiths, A. (1984) *Parent, Teacher, Child*, Methuen.

Merttens, R. and Vass, J., ibid.

Hannon, P. (1995) *Literacy, Home and School*, Falmer Press.

5 See Topping and Wolfendale (ibid.) for details of all these projects.

6 *The Norman Thomas Report on Primary Education* (1984) ILEA.

7 Walberg, H.J. and Majoribanks, K. (1976) 'Family environment and cognitive development', *Review of Educational Research*, pp 46, 527–551, National Commission on Education, Paul Hamlyn Foundation.

8 Grotberg, E. 'The Parental Role in Education and Child Development', in Dioxedes, S. (Ed.) (1979) *The Child in the World of Tomorrow*, Pergamon Press.

9 Bastiani, J. (1989) *Working with Parents: A Whole-school Approach*, NFER-Nelson.

CHAPTER 1

THE EARLY YEARS AND PARENTAL INVOLVEMENT

Every time we talk, we give order to the world.
Bakhtin

Almost 100 per cent of young children learn to talk (whether verbally or through signs). This fact seems so obvious to us most of the time that we forget to *remark* it, to see just what an achievement this is. Children are not taught to talk; no-one sits them down and says, 'Right, we did nouns yesterday and today we'll do verbs.' Indeed, there is a saying among those concerned in education which goes, 'It's just as well we don't have to teach children how to talk because if we did, 50 per cent of them would never learn!' Between the second and the fifth years of life, children master almost all the phonological and syntactical rules of their mother tongue, although they could not, of course, articulate a single one of those rules. And almost *all* children manage this extraordinary feat, not only those who are later successful at school. Only those children who are faced with an exceptional degree of handicap, or who are deprived of the chance to participate in a 'language community', fail to acquire their mother tongue within the usual timespan.

So how do children learn to talk? Who teaches them, or at least supports their learning, and can anything be said about the ways in which this process occurs? Over the last 50 years there have been a number of theories concerning language acquisition. Some of these have come from linguists – those who are concerned with the study of language. Others have their provenance in education or in developmental psychology. In this chapter we shall consider some of these theories and then move on to consider the implications for education in the

early years. The chapter will be arranged as follows:

✦ *Language acquisition:* a discussion of some of the theories which attempt to characterise how children learn to talk.

✦ *Talking at home and at school:* how does talk that takes place at home and in school differ and what are the implications of these differences?

✦ *Pre-school playgroups and nurseries:* the necessity of bridging the gap between home and school/playgroup.

✦ *Practical suggestions:* effective strategies and mechanisms by which we can bridge this gap.

Before we start our consideration of how children acquire language, we need to consider what we mean by language, and how our view of what language is has framed the discussion as to how children acquire it.

LANGUAGE AS STRUCTURE

Language may be described as a system of signs, and a sign was defined by Pierce, a linguist writing in the 1930s, as 'that which replaces something for someone'.[1] The French socio-linguist Saussure compares the sign to a piece of paper which has two sides: one side is the 'signifier', the sound or image, and the other side is the 'signified', the concept. The relationship between the signifier and the signified is, he points out, arbitrary: that is to say, there is no necessary relationship between them. This distinction – signified/signifier – has become central to the work of many writers and thinkers who have drawn upon Saussure's work. We shall ourselves be drawing again upon this distinction in Chapter 4 of this book when we consider how children learn to write.

Saussure also formalised the important distinction between 'la langue' and 'la parole'. 'La langue', translated as 'language', is the *formal and anonymous system* of language, the system of signs which are combined according to certain laws. This system exists, as Saussure says, 'only by virtue of a sort of contract signed by members of a community'. 'La parole', translated as 'speech', is 'an individual, wilful and intelligent act'.[2] It is *language in use* – as spoken by members of the speaking community in specific and contingent

situations. As Kristeva reminds us, ''la langue' is a pre-requisite for speech to occur; but at the same time, there is no *langue* in the abstract without the occurrence of speech.'[3] Each individual, using the communal and anonymous *structure* of 'la langue', communicates her individual and *particular message* to another in that subjectivisation of language which is speech.

The tendency to view language as a structure, as a system of signs governed by certain rules which may or may not be rendered explicit, is central to the work of many linguists. Chomsky, in his critique of a behaviourist view of language acquisition, drew our attention to what he believed was a crucial feature of the process. Children learning to speak, he claimed, do not simply imitate their parents. Indeed, what is remarkable about the acquisition of language is that what the children hear from the adults around them is often fragmentary, incomplete and informal, and yet what they produce is systematically grammatical. Chomsky described the language in which children are embedded as 'degenerate', thinking of this experience as providing 'data' and the language children produce as being nevertheless 'systematic at every stage'. Therefore, he argues, the behaviourist view, with its emphasis on imitation, is 'radically incomplete' as an explanation for how children learn to talk.

Instead, Chomsky suggests that the fundamental rules of all languages (the structure of 'la langue') do not have to be learned. They are part of each child's 'genetically transmitted inheritance. We are born to speak in the same way that we are born to walk upright – though we do neither for some months after birth'.[4] When a child hears language, this experience functions like a switch which starts a whole complex and essential process. Chomsky termed this 'switch' the 'Language Acquisition Device', and suggested that children treat what they hear as data from which they are able to infer the rest of the system. They will then test and refine their inferences, and so build up a tacit, *though not explicit*, understanding of the complete structure. This theory, with its dependence upon an inherited aspect (the LAD, as the Language Acquisition Device came to be labelled), profoundly influenced the character and direction of the work on children's learning to speak for more than 20 years.

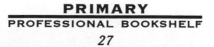

HOW CHILDREN LEARN TO SPEAK

Many developmental psychologists followed Chomsky's line in agreeing that the basis of language acquisition could not simply be imitation. However, being primarily concerned with children growing into adults rather than with language as a structure, they were more inclined to focus on 'la parole' rather than 'la langue' and to chart the details of actual children learning to speak in real homes! This shift from seeing the child as a 'little linguist' to construing him/her as an active participant in a conversational culture is exemplified by M. Halliday's study of his son Nigel's acquisition of language, *Learning How to Mean*.

Halliday charted Nigel's progress from a way of speaking which had sound and meaning but no grammar (pre-linguistic) to one where he acquired the elements of grammar and became an active participant in dialogue with others. Halliday describes Nigel's developing language in terms of its functions, suggesting that it had one minor and two major functions. The two major functions he labelled the 'active' function and the 'pragmatic' function. The minor function was the 'imaginative' function. These developed out of the conversational interactions between Nigel and his family, and Halliday believed them to be prototypes of the functions of adult language. In *Learning How to Mean*, Halliday implies that it is the constraints and affordances of specific situations which play a fundamental role in helping children learn to speak. They are not linguists but partners in a conversation.

The Bristol Language Development Project was set up by Gordon Wells and his associates in the '70s, with the explicit aim of studying a large number of children across a range of different circumstances. It was hoped to establish whether, if children learn to speak by being embedded in social interaction, there are any features of this interaction which facilitate, or mitigate against, this acquisition of language. As David Wood summarises it, 'Simply because the child is active, constructive and generative in her recreation of language it does not follow that others cannot be more or less helpful and facilitative or unhelpful and inhibiting along the way.'[5]

The findings of the Bristol Project do provide evidence for the idea that parents and other care-givers can, and do, make a difference in the ways Wood describes. Nonetheless, Wells and the others were anxious to dissociate themselves from the view that 'conditions of material poverty, and the unfavourable circumstances that belong with it, are in any direct or inevitable way associated with delayed or unsatisfactory language development.'[6]

Bruner takes the description of how children learn to talk into a new dimension in his book *Child's Talk*. Like Chomsky before him, he feels that 'imitation is a lame explanation'.[7] He also points out that the mastery of grammatical structures is 'always instrumental to doing something with words in the real world, if only *meaning* something.' The book is his study of how children learn to refer and to mean, and in this sense only it harks back to Halliday. However, Bruner is adamant in his view that language acquisition is fundamentally a matter of generating, communicating, and constituting a shared reality through the realisation of individual and shared communicative intentions.

Bruner asserts the importance of *response*, as opposed to imitation. Mothers, and other primary care-givers, crucially respond to their infants. He cites Tom Bower's work showing that an unresponsive face soon produces tears, and that withholding response is a sure-fire way to cause disruption to an infant behaviour sequence such as feeding. In developing his own characterisation of how children learn to speak, Bruner draws upon the work of two philosophers: Austin and Wittgenstein. One of Wittgenstein's most famous sayings that *'the meaning of a word is its use'*. Wittgenstein argued that it is impossible to conceive of meaning outside the context in which what is meant is spoken. Indeed, he went on to state that of what we cannot speak, we must perforce be silent: 'The limits of our language are the limits of our world.' Through our utterances we create shared meanings, and these constitute a reality for us. Communication, and indeed comprehension, are dependent upon the construction of this shared reality. Wittgenstein pointed out that even if a lion could speak, we could not understand what it said; we have no shared experiences out of which meanings may be constituted.

Austin, the other philosopher whose writing Bruner considers seminal in this context, talked about 'speech acts'. He suggested that language is formative – i.e. that we 'do things with words'.[8] Language is used not only to enable us to refer to things, to represent them when they are not there, but also to change the world, to move it around and construct a new reality. Thus when a child says, 'Gimme dat!', she is hoping to generate a new situation in which she has the desired object! Austin also argued that the meaning of an utterance cannot be analysed outside its contingent use in a specific situation, and that this analysis must take account of the *intentions* of the participants. These intentions are produced and interpreted in terms of social and linguistic conventions and thus, speech acts may be seen as grounded in these conventions. We are not usually asking for information when we say, 'Why don't you sit down?'

Bruner's study focused on two children, Richard and Jonathan, who were observed and videotaped at weekly or more frequent intervals for a period of around 20 months. Bruner divides his study into three aspects of language development and considers each in turn.

✦ *Play and games:* Bruner comments on the game-like nature of a great deal of early talk. He cites the classic 'peekaboo' game as a model for this 'playful' context in which the child learns to speak the appropriate words. At first, the mother is the primary agent in the game. It is she who hides her face and then reveals it again, uttering the word 'Peekaboo' as she does so. However, gradually the child takes a more active role, and becomes the one who hides, finally taking over the control of the game altogether. It is language as a controlling factor which Bruner highlights here. 'Russian students of language development like Luria have made much of the importance of bringing "impulsive" action under the control of language. And certainly that is the history of Jonathan, moving from the "grabbiness" of the six-month-old to the highly tuned participation of the year-old. But it is more than language that operates as a controlling factor. It is convention, negotiated conventional ways of proceeding in the game, that dominates.' So, he argues, it is the conventionalised *format* of the game which acts as the stimulus, the context and the ground of the child's developing talk.

✦ *The referring function of language:* Bruner's concern here is with the focusing of joint attention. The child makes a grasping gesture, and the parent interprets this as an intentional movement towards an object.

The object – given a name – becomes the focus of their joint attention. The movement is interpreted as 'goal-directed'. Reference, says Bruner, is 'a form of social interaction having to do with the management of joint attention.' The child initially uses non-standard, but interpretable (by the parent), sounds to produce this object-directed attention, but gradually he comes to utilise the standard forms of reference. The child does not merely imitate the mother's words: he produces the word *in response to* what his mother says. 'He is responding to the *intent* of his mother's question. He rarely mirrors her label.' (Bruner's emphasis.) The achievement of the ability to refer, Bruner concludes, depends upon the child's conversational skills and competencies rather than upon his ability to link a sound with an object in the world. The starting-point is always the achievement of joint attention, and is always embedded in a socially constructed and shared conversational reality.

◆ *The ability to pose requests:* What emerges from Bruner's study is that requesting, like referring, originates in social interaction. He describes three types of request: requests for objects, invitations where the parent's participation in a game or activity is requested, and requests for help or support. In all three, the mother has what Bruner calls an informal teaching role. She helps the child to conform to the conventions of framing requests. Replies like 'No, you can do that yourself' or 'That's not a nice noise. I'm not giving anything to you if you make that noise' help the child to master the cultural conditions of requesting and to conform to these. As with referring, the mother constantly moves the child on, demanding just a little more each time than the child has yet done. Learning how to request is not, Bruner reminds us, just 'learning language'. It is learning a culture and *'how to get things done in that culture'*.

For Bruner, then, language acquisition may be construed as the by-product of the transmission of culture. 'People are not melancholy because they invented Hell. They invented Hell because they were melancholy. Children begin to use language, by the same token, not because they have a language-using capacity, but *because they need to get things done by its use*. Parents assist them in like spirit: they want to help them become civilised human beings...' (my emphasis). In helping children learn to talk, Bruner concludes that parents do several things.

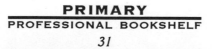

Firstly, he says, they provide *formats*. Bruner lays great stress on these formats, which he characterises as specialised versions of contexts – a 'standardised initially micro-cosmic interaction pattern between an adult and an infant that contains demarcated roles that eventually become reversed'. These routines, in which the child is at first given a role and then gradually comes to take a role of his own, and hence to control the interaction, deserve, so Bruner tells us (using Joyce's phrase), the term 'epiphanies of the ordinary. They have a script-like quality that involves not only action but a place for communication that constitutes, directs and completes the action.' These formats soon become detached from their moorings in a particular context or situation and turn into free-floating frameworks for new sets of activity. The transactions which take place retain their familiar character, but within the context of a new venture. Thus the social and linguistic competencies of the child are extended and generalised by the format beyond its original setting.

Secondly, parents utilise formats in order to create shared referential contexts. In helping children to develop their ability to refer, the mother operates a type of 'fine-tuning' mechanism. At first, she restricts both the actions and the vocabulary within a recognised format to those which she believes the child can handle. Gradually, as he progresses, she makes more demands and in turn responds at a higher level. But the aim of her fine-tuning is not simply a refinement of the child's language. 'The child is being trained, not only to know the language, but *to use it as a member of a cultural community*.'

Thirdly, the mother provides a continuity of social processes such as turn-taking, role interchange, verbal entrance and exit rituals (i.e. how we begin and end conversations), and so on. The child's early language acquisition depends heavily upon the construction and use of a shared context, and upon the familiarity of this context and the conventions by which the verbal interactions take place. Throughout this discussion, Bruner emphasises the importance of the formats, those routinised and repeated language interactions where parents and infants do things to and with each other. Such formats, he claims, 'are crucial vehicles in the passage from communication to language'.

In summary, it may be said that language acquisition and the transmission of culture are now seen as intrinsically related. The process of learning to talk is a process of enculturation, and the work which developmental psychologists and educationalists are currently engaged in attempts to provide further and more detailed descriptions of the precise nature of the mechanisms involved. Children learn to speak through *responding* to situations in which they are treated as conversational partners. Imitation is a part of this process, but it is not through imitating or repeating that children acquire language: it is through interpreting, and responding to, the intentions of others within a shared and familiar context.

FROM HOME TO SCHOOL...

Alongside the work which has been done in attempting to characterise children's acquisition of language, there has been a focus on the differences between talk at home and talk in the classroom. This focus has been at least partly motivated by the concern that children from particular types of socio-economic background are less likely to succeed at school than others from a different type of background. The work of three different people or groups comes to mind here, and we shall briefly summarise the points made by each one.

1. Bernstein: The most influential and important work into this relationship has been done by Bernstein. Bernstein's major insight was to provide a sociological explanation, at the level of theory, which demonstrated the link between forms of speech on the one hand and socio-economic class on the other. Bernstein argued that the form of speech, the ways in which things are said and the framing of what is said, are both indicative and formative of particular types of social relationship. This means that different subcultures in society will utilise different forms of speech, which will themselves then act to reproduce those subcultures. The terminology which Bernstein used to characterise these differences has led to many contentious readings of his work, which he has been at pains to repudiate.

Bernstein contrasts two forms of speech, which he describes as 'codes': restricted code and elaborated code. Children from less socio-economically advantaged backgrounds are more likely to be embedded in

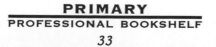

a restricted code, while those from the better-off homes are more likely to use an elaborated code. Users of restricted codes are more likely to speak in a way which assumes that the listener is familiar with the context of what they are saying; they are likely to use terms such as 'this', 'that', 'those' and so on, and to leave the shared aspects of the speaking situation tacit rather than making them explicit. Users of elaborated codes are likely to spell things out, speaking as if the listener were unaware of the physical and social context of the speaker. They will make things explicit rather than leaving them tacit, and will use verbal rather than gestural means to refer to things.

Bernstein has been at pains to insist that no value judgement is intended in the use of these particular terms to categorise these codes. He suggests that the restricted code implies the elliptical, inexplicit use of language which may facilitate a warm and intimate communication, in contrast with the interpersonal distance created and maintained by the very explicitness of the elaborated code. However, the implicit assumption that restricted code use acts to disadvantage children from 'working class' backgrounds has clearly influenced a whole variety of programmes whose stated aim is to repair or remediate the 'damage' caused by their being embedded in a more 'restricted' culture. The deficit model of parenting implied has resulted in a great deal of criticism of Bernstein's terminology. Many people feel strongly that his work has been used to locate the causes of disadvantage emphatically in the family and the community rather than in the structures of the educational system.

2. *Tizard and Hughes:* This study utilised tape recordings and observations made of thirty four-year-old girls in nursery school in the morning and at home with their mothers in the afternoon. The main aim of the research was the comparison of the nature and quality of children's learning at home and at school. Although the authors expressed their conviction that nursery schools and classes 'provide a secure and enjoyable environment in which young children can play, and explore the wider social world beyond the home',[9] nonetheless they felt that it was unlikely that the nursery environment would be linguistically and intellectually richer than the home, in terms of the stimulation it offered children. The presupposition that this is so was, they felt, based on little if any empirical evidence.

The findings of the research bore out this suspicion. The transcripts revealed the home to be an extraordinarily rich environment in linguistic terms. And the study found no evidence that conversations in the working-class homes were any less prolific or stimulating than those in the middle-class homes. There were differences, but they were differences of style rather than quality. The authors repudiated the idea of any 'language deficit' in working-class homes, claiming that in all homes there was a wide range of language usage. However, when it came to the analysis of the same children talking in their nursery surroundings, the situation was very different. 'The conversations [of the children] with their teachers made a sharp contrast to those with their mothers. The richness, depth and variety which characterised the home conversations was sadly missing. So too was the sense of intellectual struggle, and of the real attempts being made to communicate on both sides.' The authors also commented that these differences between home and school were particularly pronounced in the case of the working-class children. Compared to the middle-class children, they were 'more likely to be subdued, to play a passive role in conversations and to avoid asking questions of the nursery staff'.

The findings of this study do not refute Bernstein's theory of a relationship between social class and forms of speech. Indeed, they bear out the notion that children from particular types of home are less familiar with, and therefore less competent in, the styles of conversation and dialogue utilised most commonly at school. However, they do, importantly, give the lie to those readings of Bernstein which see working-class homes as deficient, or less effective, in terms of the educational and intellectual environment they provide. Indeed, the study was widely reported as implying that children were better left at home rather than being sent to nursery – an implication refuted vigorously by the authors.

3. *The Bristol Language Development Project:* This project, mentioned earlier in the chapter, produced findings which concurred, to a large extent, with those of the Tizard and Hughes study. Wells, and his colleagues, found no class-correlated differences between quality or styles of speech in the home. 'There were no obvious differences in style of adult or child speech which would tend to support the theory

of strongly class-associated differences in code. In fact, in all homes the range and level of conversation was for the most part highly dependent on context and restricted to familiar everyday experiences.'[10] However, on entry to school, differences do appear in the children's ability to cope with the context of the classroom, and these differences are class-related. Wells concludes that there is no justification for 'forming expectations about children's oral language abilities on entry to school that are based solely upon their parents' membership in a certain social class.'

Wells characterised specific factors which, he felt, aided the processes of language acquisition and of intellectual growth in general. He, and his colleagues, distinguished between a 'supportive' style of conversational interaction, and a 'didactic' style. In the former, the adult encourages the child to initiate a conversation, acknowledges what she says, requires her to elaborate upon it and allows the 'ownership' of the conversation to rest with the child. In the latter, the choice of topic is more usually the adult's, the mode of dialogue is commonly question and answer (where a limited range of responses is expected and demanded from the child), and the adult not infrequently feeds the child's mistakes back to her. Wells does acknowledge the value of both styles, but finds that a prevalence of the former are more likely to be associated with enhanced linguistic competence at an earlier age. Clearly, the former style is much more commonly associated with language in the home, whereas the latter is correlated with language in the school.

WHAT ARE THE IMPLICATIONS OF THIS?

Research on how children learn to talk, and subsequently on the structural differences between home and school, clearly has implications for how we, as teachers in playgroups and nurseries, work with both the children and their parents. To tease out these implications, let us summarise what we have learned from the thinkers and writers mentioned above:

1. Learning to talk

✦ Children acquire language in a process of enculturation. They may be said to be 'embedded in language', and are treated as conversational partners from early infancy.

✦ Together with their parents, children occupy and construct a shared conversational reality. This is crucial. As Wittgenstein points out, without such a common ground of experience and perception no common language is possible.

✦ Imitation is only one partial aspect of the process of learning to speak. *Response*, however, is central, as is the adult mediation provided.

✦ Mothers and other primary care-givers provide *formats* or structures into which children's first steps in talking are fitted. These formats enable the child to move from a passive and responsive role to that of active initiator.

✦ Children learning to speak are learning *how to do things with words*. They are becoming active members of a culture. In this sense, it is language as 'parole', as contingent speaking acts, with which we as teachers must be concerned rather than language as 'langue', as a system of grammatical or syntactical rules and structures.

2. At home...

✦ *Children learn to talk at home*. All homes provide a rich source of linguistic and intellectual stimulation for the developing speaker.

✦ There may be differences between homes in terms of speaking style, in terms of the modalities, the tonalities and the framing of what is said, although Wells' data from the BLDP does not bear this out entirely. But there is no suggestion that the quality of talk is any less, nor that children learn to speak any slower or less effectively in working-class homes than in middle-class homes.

3. At school....

✦ There are important differences between the nature and style of conversations in the home and at school. Talk at home is largely contingent upon immediate happenings or events; it is often child-initiated and led; it may have an elliptical and deictic[11] character. Talk at school tends to be adult-led and focused. It is often more didactic in character, depending upon a question/answer mode. The length of the conversation, its focus and content, and the range of possible child-responses are all more prescribed than they are at home.

✦ There is evidence that working-class children find the move from home to school more disruptive in terms of their language development than do their middle-class counterparts.

✦ Children's educational performance at age 10 correlates strongly with their socio-economic class, and this correlation is even stronger by the time they reach age 16.

The implications of all this are not hard to elaborate. Parents are, in a very real sense, their children's first educators. For many years, it has been assumed that it is parents who need educating (by professionals) and that 'they' have a lot to learn from 'us'. Tizard and Hughes conclude their book by suggesting that 'it is time to shift the emphasis away from what parents should learn from professionals, and towards what professionals can learn from studying parents and children at home.' And as teachers, we can learn a lot from listening to what parents say – not only about their own children's interests, anxieties, strengths and weaknesses, but also about the values and approaches of the community of which they are a part.

We can also see the effects of the structural differences between homes and school in terms of children's learning. The nature and the quality of the talk at home and in the classroom are not commensurate. The question 'How many ____ are there?' appears to be the same question whether it is uttered at home or in school, and whatever is being counted. However, we know that this is not the case. If I ask a child to thread some beads on to a string in class or playgroup, and then I ask them 'How many beads have you threaded?', the child knows that this is not a request for information. They know that I know how many beads there are on that string. They realise that actually the question is a covert demand for them to count, and that I am asking them if they know *how* to count correctly.

By contrast, if I ask my son at home, 'How many chocolate biscuits are there left in that tin?' he knows that this is definitely a request for information – I do actually want to know the answer. In the first case, the schoolchild knows that a number of strategies for answering that question are not open to her. For example, she can't turn to her neighbour and say, 'She wants to know how many beads I've threaded. Can you count them for me.' She must answer for herself. However, my son may well yell to his sister, 'Annie, Mum wants to know how many chocolate biscuits are left!' And in the former situation there would be no point in lying, while in the latter there might be very good reason to do so! Although the question is *grammatically* the same in both contexts, and it may even contain exactly the same words, we can see that, considered as a *speech utterance*, it is simply not the same question. Different strategies may well be employed to answer it, and different resources are drawn upon in each case.

It is easy to see how difficult some children find the move into this new context of the playgroup or classroom if we look at videotapes of children who have newly arrived in this situation. Mary Willes gives an example in her book *Children into Pupils* (1983) of a reception teacher reading a story to a group of four-year-olds. She stops reading the story and asks the class to look at the picture. 'How many claws can we see on the pussycat's paw?' The children look but no-one offers an answer. She repeats the question, and still no-one volunteers an answer. She chooses a child, and asks him, 'Jatinder, how many claws has the cat got, do you think?' The child replies, 'Three.' The teacher pauses, and once again draws his attention to the picture, repeating her question. This time Jatinder replies, 'Four.' 'Yes!' responds the teacher, very pleased that he has answered correctly. 'And how did you know it was four, Jatinder?' 'Cos I'm four!' says Jatinder, and the other children all chip in. 'I'm four too!', 'My sister's three', 'I'm four!', and so on.

We can see what the teacher is after here. She wants to use the story as the stimulation for a small counting exercise. This seems a very sensible and reasonable aim. But we can also see what the children are doing. They have already accumulated quite a lot of knowledge about how conversations go in school. They know that when the teacher asks a question, just one person has to answer it. They also know that you are not supposed to ask your friends for help, but must answer alone. Furthermore, Jatinder recognises that the answer to a 'how many' question is a number. He hurls a number into the situation – 'Three!' This doesn't go down very well. He hurls another number in. This one goes down well. Then he is asked to account for the second number, so he thinks of a good reason for saying that number. 'I'm four!' But this is not what the teacher wants to hear. We can see how the *style* of conversation and its framing, the conditions under which utterances can be made and accepted, all act to preclude the more helpful and stimulating conversation of the less-formalised home context.

BRIDGING THE GAP

It must be accepted that, for good reasons, most children spend a proportion of their pre-school years in an institutional educational setting such as a nursery or playgroup. So how do we bridge the gap between home and school, between parents and teachers?

Gordon Wells alerts our attention to the central importance of literacy in this connection. He points out that children from working-class backgrounds may be said to be linguistically disadvantaged on entry to school, but *not* in relation to their command of spoken language and their ability to communicate orally. We have commented upon this earlier in the chapter. Their disadvantage, he maintains, may be located in the attainment of something he terms 'literacy'. We shall discuss precisely what *literacy* signifies, and the implications of various interpretations of the term, in Chapter 4. But for now, we are simply concerned with the implications of Wells' statements for teachers in nurseries and playgroups.

Wells found that the children's level of literacy on entry to school correlated strongly with overall achievement at age seven and also at age eleven. Thus the literacy levels of young children may be viewed as a good predictor of educational success. These findings, and Wells' commentary on them, articulate a common-sense view held by many teachers. We often feel that it is the experiences children have had, or have not had, in their pre-school years which dictate, at least in part, their achievement once they get to school. However, previously the focus of this feeling has mostly been on children's ability to communicate orally, i.e. on their attainment in terms of the acquisition of spoken language. This we must now recognise to be misplaced. It is not children's ability to talk which is in question, although we should recognise the important differences which may exist in the styles and forms of speech in different communities. We must look elsewhere for the sources of their disadvantage.

The Headstart programme in the USA was an attempt to address the perceived disadvantage of children from poor or working-class homes. Much of the programme concerned itself with the provision of books and other resources useful for developing children's literacy. The results of Headstart have been well disseminated and it is widely accepted that the programme does succeed, to a degree, in breaking the correlation between socio-economic background and children's attainment at age ten. However, this programme and others like it have come in for a certain amount of criticism on the basis that the sources of disadvantage are once again so firmly located in the home.

The argument made by many who research and practise in the field of early childhood education is that currently schools place a very high value on literacy and, concomitantly, upon the ability to think reflectively about experience and also about texts. Donaldson refers to the emphasis placed by teachers on 'disembedded' thinking. 'What is required for success in our educational system is that [the child] should learn to turn language and thought upon themselves. He must become able to direct his own thought processes in a thoughtful manner. He must be able not just to talk, but to choose what to say; not just to interpret, but to weigh possible interpretations... He must become capable of manipulating symbols.'[12]

Children need not only to be able to speak – they can all do this – but also to reflect upon what was said and how it was said. They need to be able to think textually, to create and examine texts of their own and others' making.

Stories, we can now be certain from the evidence of both research and practice, play a major role in helping children to develop these abilities. Not only Wells and Tizard and Hughes, but Frank Smith, with his notion of 'literacy clubs', Rosen and Rosen, the Bullock Report and a whole host of other writers including a recent book by Carol Fox, have all stressed the central importance of stories in this regard. Fox stresses the role stories play in helping children to learn in many different ways. She says that there are 'many kinds of knowledge that are borne along on the back of stories... stories [told by children] carry with them their classificatory systems, their forms of reasoning and argument, their observations of natural and physical laws, their concepts of number, shape, size, and so on, even their awareness of moral and metaphysical possibilities... All kinds of storying involve the story-teller in the organisation of knowledge structures.'[13]

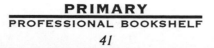

All of this adds up to make an argument for a much closer alignment of home and school, where parents and teachers together encourage children by telling, reading and discussing stories, and by allowing children to tell their own stories. It matters little whether these stories are anecdotal-based on incidents and events experienced by the children themselves or those around them – or whether they are 'literary' in the traditional sense of the term. What is essential is that the stories and conversations children tell and have at home are not disconnected, in terms of style, format and content, from those which teachers use and expect from children at school.

PRACTICAL SUGGESTIONS

There are many pragmatic suggestions which can be made, following directly from this discussion. We can highlight what is important in terms of influencing children's achievement – particularly if we are, as teachers and as educators, interested in breaking the connection between achievement and socio-economic class or race. Up front, in terms of both policy and practice in playgroups, nurseries and infant classes, should be the following items:

✦ The awareness that children from *all* social and ethnic backgrounds are likely to come into school from an environment which has provided a rich source of linguistic and intellectual stimulation.

✦ The importance of talking and listening to parents about their children's interests, how they learn best, their idiosyncrasies and their preferences.

✦ The importance of involving parents in classroom story-reading sessions.

✦ The necessity for books to be taken home from school and, where possible, for 'home' books to come into school.

There are various ways in which these can be implemented. We have categorised the range of options available to schools and playgroups under the following headings: Home visits, Booklet for parents, Activities and books for parents and children to share, Games libraries, Parent networks and Parent rooms.

1. Home visits

Many schools have found ways of making time for the reception or nursery teacher to visit the homes of the children who are about to start school. All those who engage in this practice report how worthwhile it is, from the point of view of both the teacher and of the child. The teacher is meeting the child on his own ground, in his 'territory' (so to speak) and this makes an enormous difference to the quality of the interaction. The teacher can obtain a sense of the home environment, and of its culture. She can able to be shown where the child sleeps, see his favourite toys and find out about his interests. Children often talk about this visit for many days, and regard it as an important event. Teachers almost unanimously describe in positive terms the usefulness of the visit, and how much they are able to learn.

Most schools 'fund' these visits through a system of some supply cover and some directed time. The length of the visits is normally 20 minutes or so, although of course some do 'run over'! Therefore, with an afternoon's or morning's supply cover, a teacher can fit in three or four visits. Most schools spread out the visits over the half-term immediately preceding the children's entry to school, and set them up either when the parents look round the school or during a 'New Parents' Meeting' held early in the half-term before the children start.

The 'New Parents' Meeting' is also a very helpful and valuable event connected to these home visits. The meeting is usually very relaxed, with the parents and the teacher meeting over a cup of tea or coffee immediately after school or in the evening. The meeting provides an opportunity for the teacher to run through the mechanics of the school day and week, explaining which day is PE day, when swimming is organised, what time lunch is, how the lunch-hour is divided, where the children eat their lunch, and so on. Perhaps, unsurprisingly, it is the simple 'what' and 'when' aspects of school life which parents need to know, and which are prone to cause a great deal of trouble if information is not provided. At the meeting, teachers and parents together arrange the time for the home visit.

At the meeting, or during the visit to the parent's home, the parents should be encouraged to talk to the teacher about their – and the child's – expectations of school. Perhaps a child has seen an older sister or brother start school. This may have given them particular expectations and it is important that these are addressed, particularly if the circumstances are now different or the school has changed. For example, in one case, a child had an older sister who had learned to read using a particular set of books. She had loved listening to the stories in this particular scheme, and had confidently imagined that when she started school, she too would be reading these books. She was most disappointed to discover that the teachers had changed schemes, and no longer used those stories! This led to many arguments between the teacher and the child and, subsequently, between the teacher and the parents. This is exactly the sort of thing that can be sorted out at a pre-starting-school meeting or during a home visit. In this particular case, the first reading scheme was still in the school and could have been used alongside the new one if the teacher had realised the significance, of those particular books to the child.

2. Booklet for parents

The crucial thing about this booklet is that it should be short, illustrated, and easy to read. It is immensely helpful to involve some parents in the writing of it, and to take their advice as to the things they feel they need to know or were most puzzled about. Many parents are more concerned about whether the child can go to the toilet during the periods between playtimes, or what they need to wear for PE, than they are about the maths curriculum or the school policy on religious assemblies. The booklet can provide a list of the sorts of things the child will be expected to be able to do on entry to school – dress themselves, do up their buttons, go to the toilet, write their names, eat with a knife and fork, and so on. A way in which it can be even more helpful is if it can provide some simple activities for parents and children to share to help the children learn to read and write their names, count to ten and recognise numbers.

The good 'Starting School' booklets produced by schools for parents have, in one way or another, incorporated the following:

✦ An outline of the school day – what happens when.

✦ An outline of the week – when PE, assemblies, library sessions and so on take place.

✦ The dates of the terms, together with the dates of any school outings, school fairs, discos, jumble sales.

✦ A list of things the child is expected to be able to do on entry into school. (Don't make it too long or too intimidating!)

✦ Some references to books, games or activities which are useful resources for parents – Snakes and Ladders, *We're Going on a Bear Hunt*, and so on.

✦ Illustrations – preferably drawn by the children themselves.

The booklet can be given to all the parents who come to the 'New Parents Meeting' and then, subsequently, to parents on home visits. Any parents who neither come nor are visited should get one anyway.

3. Activities and books for parents and children to share

Many schools are starting to send home books on a 'library-lending' basis even before the children actually start school. In addition, they supply a few activities for the children and their parents to share at home in preparation for starting school. This helps the child to be ready to start school, both psychologically and cognitively. Many good activities may be found in the early years books produced by the IMPACT Project, and ideas can also be culled from other resource books.

The advantages of sending a small 'pack' of activities for children and parents to do together are manifold. The children start to feel like they are 'schoolchildren', and are likely to make progress with some of the 'basic' starting skills – reading and writing their names, counting to ten and recognising the numbers, letter recognition, drawing and cutting skills, and so on. Secondly, the school can select the activities for its pack to reflect the approach of the school. Therefore, if the teachers are anxious that parents do not press their children on certain skills but do share other activities, they can focus the pack in that direction. Thirdly, the parents' relationship with the school starts off with the feeling that their support and the things that they do with their children are not only valued but are an intrinsic part of their child's education.

4. Games libraries

It is inevitable that many parents of nursery- or reception-aged children will have younger siblings to cope with. This often means that they feel that the amount of help they can offer the class teacher or the school is limited. Perhaps it means that they cannot help in the classroom, listening to readers or sharing games with the children, even though they might wish to do so. However, there are many ways in which they can help that do not involve spending long periods in the school. There are some very good IMPACT and shared writing games, and several other books of more general literacy games, which are presented in the form of photocopiable sheets. These are not very appealing to children; and yet, if enlarged and then coloured with paint or felt-tipped pens, they can be extremely attractive.

In quite a number of schools, teachers have managed to organise a group of parents who 'make' games – not in the sense of creating them, but in the sense of reproducing them. These games can then be organised into a 'games library', and parents and children can take it in turns to borrow these, either before the children start school or once they have already started. A simple signing-in and out procedure is usually all that is required, and there is normally a time-limit on how long a person can keep a particular game. Some schools also provide resources, such as counters and dice, which may be borrowed with the games. Other schools prefer to run a system whereby they buy in lots of dice (the ten-sided variety are wonderful!) at a low price from an educational supplier, and sell them on to parents to cover their costs. They can also do the same thing with small packs of five crayons, with adhesive tape and Pritt sticks, card, and so on. Making materials available cheaply to parents is often a very important part of helping parents to share activities and encourage children's work at home.

5. Parent networks

It is important to help parents of new children in the school feel that they are part of a community. One of the simplest ways of doing this is to set up a parent network. The teacher can put together a list of all the children in the class, with the names of their parents and their phone numbers. If people do not want to be on the list, they can elect not to; but it is best to suggest that in the absence of an objection, their names will be included. Such a list greatly facilitates parents getting in touch with each other, helping their children develop friendships and being able to follow these up. A class list is a simple device, but it is extraordinary how much it can help to achieve that sense of community.

6. Parent rooms

In recent years, many schools have been fortunate in that they have applied for, and obtained, the resources to set up a 'parent room' in the school. Nowadays, the sources for such extra funding may have dried up

completely or at least been greatly reduced in number. However, setting up a parent room is still an option which many schools may want to consider, especially if they have some extra or under-utilised space.

The room does not need to be large, or particularly well-equipped. Essential items include chairs, a fridge, some store cupboards, a kettle and – most importantly – a noticeboard! There needs to be a supply of second-hand toys, as many books as possible and a system for maintaining a supply of coffee, tea, biscuits and juice for the little ones! Once the room is set up, it can serve many purposes. These will depend in large part upon the nature of the community in which the school is located and its specific needs, but they may include the following:

✦ Providing a safe warm space where mothers can gather for a cup of tea/coffee and get out of the house with their children. This can be the difference between surviving and not surviving as a parent, particularly in areas of social and economic disadvantage.

✦ Opening up the school to the wider community.

✦ Housing a toys and games library.

✦ Allowing mothers to run an 'exchange programme' for small children's clothing and equipment such as pushchairs.

✦ Fostering a network of parents – especially through the use of the noticeboard for messages.

✦ Holding adult or community education classes or courses – often run and organised by the local adult or community education services. These can include anything from English lessons for bilingual parents to aerobics for all and sundry.

✦ Providing a familiar and welcoming environment for meetings.

Anyone who has ever been in a school where there is a flourishing parent room can attest to its value. These things are hard to quantify but the benefits reside not only in the increased sense of fellowship among the parents, but also in a more effective relationship between the institutions of home and school. Both teachers and parents know where to find each other; if teachers need help – on a school outing, with some resources, for a sporting event – they can discuss their needs over a cup of coffee, on the parents' own ground. There is no better way of saying that we believe parents to be an important part of a school, and that their role in children's education is essential, than by giving them a named room.

CONCLUSIONS

In children's early years, their parents are the major source of their education and support in facilitating their learning. The environment of the home provides a rich source of linguistic and intellectual stimulation. Conversations in the home are lively interchanges in which children frequently play not only an active but a leading role. Schools cannot emulate this context, nor should they try to do so. Teachers can, and do, introduce children to a wide range of subject matter and speech forms which are not necessarily or commonly available to them at home. However, it behoves us to bear in mind that for many children the entrance into school is not only a change of physical and social situation and customs. It also involves a completely new set of routines, conventions and ways of speaking. The more bridges we can build between home and school, the better children will be able to encompass the changes required of them.

Where there are parents in the classroom whose input is valued, where books and games travel back and forth between home and school, where parents and younger siblings have a space in the school in which they can share stories and play, the gap between home and school will appear neither as a treacherous chasm across which no-one passes nor as the opaque curtain where what happens on the 'other side' can only be guessed at. We cannot turn nurseries into homes, nor would we want to turn homes into educational institutions. But we can recognise the job that each does and value their differences as well as building on the commonality of their aims.

REFERENCES

1 Pierce, C.S. (1931) *Collected Papers*, Hartshorne & Weiss (Eds.), Harvard University Press.
2 Saussure, F. (1922) *Course in General Linguistics*, Payot.
3 Kristeva, J. (1989) *Language, the Unknown*, Columbia University Press.
4 Willes, M. (1983) *Children into Pupils*, Routledge and Kegan Paul.
5 Wood, D. (1988) *How Children Think and Learn*, Blackwell.
6 Willes, M., ibid.
7 Bruner, J. (1983) *Child's Talk: Learning to use language*, Oxford University Press.

8 Austin, J. (1962) *How to Do Things with Words*, Oxford University Press.

9 Tizard, B. and Hughes, M. (1984) *Young Children Learning*, Fontana.

10 Wells, G. (1986) *The Meaning Makers*, Hodder & Stoughton.

11 The word 'Deixis' is a Greek word meaning 'to point', and deictic forms are words or expressions which point to or in some way identify people or things which are not actually named. For example, words like 'this' or 'that' point to things which are not named; 'I' or 'you' are words whose meaning depends upon who is uttering them. Thus deictic words depend totally for their meaning upon the context of their utterance.

12 Donaldson, M. (1978) *Children's Minds*, Fontana.

13 Fox, C. (1993) *At the Very Edge of the Forest*, Cassell.

READING: THE INVOLVEMENT OF PARENTS

From T-shirts to bubble gum wrappers, children live in a world fashioned in print. Few can escape the abundance of words that fill their homes, and yet we know very little about that world or its effects on learning to read and write in schools...

Denny Taylor

INTRODUCTION

Parental involvement can be configured and practised in a variety of ways. Some schools consider parental involvement to mean sending reading books home with the children and expecting parents to read with their children – at home. For others, it means bringing parents into the school and involving them in working alongside teachers and children on literacy or other activities.

In this chapter, we will attempt to focus on some issues concerning parental involvement in reading which are framed by wider discussions relating to the social contexts of literacy learning. We will assume a certain amount of knowledge as far as the teaching and learning of reading is concerned. We will examine quite closely how *context* not only crucially influences the way literacy is mediated, but also actually defines what literacy is. By referring to some classic ethnographic studies of children's literacy development, both in this country and abroad, we will explore the nature of literacy (and reading in particular) as a social practice embedded in social contexts. We will also look at the diversifying nature of literacy in different social contexts by focusing briefly on the emergence of the notion of a 'television literacy' in the context of the home, and what implications this has for literacy learning in general. The chapter also provides a fund of practical advice on how to embark on establishing a listening dialogue with parents on curriculum issues such as reading, and how to launch and maintain a project of parental involvement in reading ,with notes for teachers to help plan parent meetings and workshops.

THE DOMAINS OF LITERACY

One of the most fruitful domains for the mediation (that is, conveyance) of texts between parent and child is the home environment: that cluster of intimate and familiar sites where parents and children socially interact and mediate literate activity to each other through the daily routines of their lives – through entertainment, school-related activity, religious practice and all the other behaviours involved in family and community life. The home is also a rich source of various artefacts of literacy such as comics, newspapers, leaflets, coupons, notes, letters, T-shirts, magazines, television, books, tickets, record sleeves/CD cases, greetings cards, computer games and food packaging. These texts are not accidentally, or haphazardly, situated in the home: they are woven into the environment of the home to establish it as a particular kind of context clearly distinct from the context of the school. (Even the word 'context' itself is interesting because it is a metaphor deriving from Latin: *con* meaning with, *text* meaning to weave.)

Another rich source for the artefacts of literacy is the local environment where, in cityscapes in particular, the most obvious physical feature is the dominance of the printed word, and where the actions and behaviour of adults and children are directly affected by the signs of shop fronts, advertising hoardings, street names, triangular traffic warnings, circular traffic commands, rectangular traffic directions, flashing prohibitions, bus destinations, clothing logos, confectionery and fast food wrappings, and many others (see the final chapter for examples of mediated literate behaviour in these contexts).

The mediation of signs in such settings involves the individual in social and often collaborative activity. Indeed, some studies both here

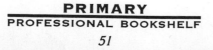

and in the United States[1] show how everyday literacy can involve the building up of complex networks of social support which include the mediation and interpretation of such things as operating a washing machine or mechanically repairing cars. Peter Hannon[2] has constructed a very useful theoretical framework which sets out ways in which teachers can help parents to recognise the opportunities for modelling literacy in various interactional contexts.

Literacy in the conventional print sense and literacy in new and evolving senses such as technical, electronic or media literacy are embedded in the social practices of the real world, and should have more of a bearing on what we, as teachers, do with literacy as a curriculum and pedagogic practice. One inspiring young teacher known to us in the East End of London has transformed the reading attitudes of his Year Six boys by importing into the classroom car manuals, car engines and car mechanics! Reflecting on the social processes of literacy in social contexts can powerfully renew and reform our professional practice. Involving children practically in this reflection, for example by documenting why, when, where and how their parents, grandparents, neighbours or role-models read and write,[3] can lead to fascinating projects on the ethnography of literacy and perhaps to forming critical views about the dynamics of its power.[4]

BEFORE SCHOOL

In order to explore these issues a little more carefully, we shall examine the 'home' and the 'school' as two sociological domains. Domains may be defined as having their own particular ways of speaking (rhetorics) and their own particular ways of behaving (practices). Within these practices come things such as rituals. Of course, we realise that 'homes' or 'schools' are not homogeneous as such. There are very many different types of home, and many different kinds of school and school approach. Differences in school approaches to reading and consequent relationships with parents will be discussed at the end of the chapter. However, despite these intra-home and intra-school variations, the domains of home and school have distinct differences – but also some surprising similarities in the area of the teaching of reading, at least to school-age children.

Peter Hannon draws an interesting table which suggests some possible differences between 'Home learning' and 'School learning'.[5]

PRACTICE: HOME READING AND SCHOOL READING

Home reading practice	School reading practice
Relaxed	More formalised
'On demand' reading – children choose which books to read and when.	Timetabled times to read. Teachers do not always have time to read when the child wants to.
Whole books are read at a time and discussed.	Only enough time to read a few pages or very short books, with quick discussions.
'Books are books' – generally no divisions are made between reading scheme and other books.	Traditional reading scheme books seen to have a specific purpose.
Child's progression informally observed.	Reading records are kept.
Attitudes towards reading and expectations	
'Non-professional'	'Professional'
Parents see reading mainly as a technical skill of decoding. For example, using the pictures thought of as 'cheating'; using flashcards and word tins very	Teachers see reading in a much wider sense; 'becoming a reader' encompasses: learning to enjoy books, making sense, being a critical reader, and decoding.

useful. Reading must involve words. Parents expect more formal decoding to be taught.	Teachers agree that there is a progression within the process of learning to read, but that this is not necessarily a linear progression.
Reading goes in stages – reading scheme books display the stages, help you keep track and make sure your child is progressing.	Reading schemes (traditional) are seen to be restricting and uninspiring, tending to introduce a competitive element into the process, which can do far more harm than good.
Parents often feel intimidated by reading diaries (e.g. as used in PACT), and do not often write in them.	Teachers expect there to be many opportunities for reading in the home, and that the reading diaries should be written in – or at least, some kind of mark should be made to show that a book has been shared with somebody.

The two domains of home and school, with their context-specific practices and rituals, offer two very different reading environments. Life at home is not the same as life at school; expectations and behaviour vary widely between the two situations.

THE DOMAIN OF THE HOME

The home environment is, generally speaking, a far more informal, more child-led environment than the school. Research has shown that children in the home environment are far more likely to be the instigators of a conversation or activity than in the more structured and organised environment of the school.[6] Children have a much closer relationship with the adults at home, who are far more available than teachers and who, at any time, can be pulled in several directions at once.

When younger children ask to read a book, it is the whole book they want to look at and talk about. They are not, or should not be, reading in order to 'practise' a skill, but to enjoy the story the book has to offer. They may share the reading of the book, the parent may read it to the child, or it may be seen as an opportunity for the child to read to the parent. A recent study in Sheffield[7] found that working-class parents, '...despite having no training were found to be using a wide range of moves within strategies that were similar in many respects to those of trained professionals.' So the strategies parents use in reading with their children appear to be very similar to those utilised by their teachers. The books that teachers might expect to appear on a child's bookshelf at home might include picture books, story compilations and non-fictional books. However, other adult literature in the home will of course play an important part in the children's literacy development. Television listings, car manuals, newspapers and address books are all kinds of reading matter that might appear in the home. The way adults use these materials, and read their own books or magazines, journals and papers, all model a certain attitude towards and behaviour in reading.

THE INFLUENCE OF THE COMMUNITY

Teachers, even well-informed ones, may not always be aware of the complexity and diversity of the home environment of individual children in their class. Shirley Brice Heath's classic ethnographic study[8] researched into three diverse communities in the southern states of the US, all of which fed into one particular primary school. She looked into children's literate traditions in the home, and consequent literacy orientation. What she found was that these literate traditions had a strong influence on the children's subsequent performance and success at school.

> How children come to read, write and talk is completely embedded in their cultural environment – the school works with a child already 'enculturated' into certain attitudes and knowledge about reading and writing.

Heath describes two of the communities – 'Tracton', a black working-class community and 'Roadville', a white working class community, both situated on the edge of a cotton mill town in the Piedmont Carolinas. Although these communities were immersed in, and surrounded by, Western mainstream culture, their literacy orientations were quite different from one another and from their neighbouring mainstream culture.

The Tracton community was of a mainly oral tradition; they nurtured their children by constantly holding and cuddling them while they were babies. The children's early attempts at making sounds were largely ignored as babies' babble. Their toys were household objects, and generally there were no books for children in the house. The adults read adult-orientated materials such as pamphlets or letters, but they did not read to the children. Heath observed very little instruction or mediation of any kind towards the children. They were expected to 'come to know' all the things that the adults already knew. Their parents 'modelled' certain behaviours, and Heath describes how, by the ages of 12–24 months, the children were very accomplished imitators of voice in intonation and parts of speech. The adults enjoyed this kind of 'mimicry' and applauded it. By the age of two and a half, most children could imitate the walk and talk of everyone in the community, and even frequent visitors such as the repair man or postman. When the children made observations, or did anything, they were not asked questions along the lines of 'What's that?' but 'What's that like?' That is to say, they were constantly being made to compare what they saw with what they knew (for example, a picture of a duck in a book was immediately connected with 'Uncle Bill's ducks on the farm'... 'How do they go?') By the time these children entered school they had developed very strong narrative skills, and were able to tell stories by 'drawing heavily on their abilities to set a stage and to call on the audience's power to join in the imaginative creation of a story'. However, these story-telling skills differed from the 'mainstream' literate traditions of the 'Once upon a time' or '...happily ever after' type. Their stories centred around 'true stories', events within their own immediate experience which they fictionalised, such as family anecdotes.

When they came to school, Tracton children found themselves unprepared for many of the practices and rituals expected of them in the classroom situation, such as stories from books (with their unrealistic illustrations), sitting still and 'getting on', working from workbooks and writing of any kind. They enjoyed stories, although they needed to interact constantly with the teacher – which was considered 'naughty'. They were good mimics, and more than likely found themselves in trouble for accurate impersonations of teachers behind their backs or in the playground. Good dramatic and improvisational skills were not recognised as valuable or useful in those schools at that time, and the children seemed doomed to failure right from the start. Heath remarks:

> ...the majority not only fail to learn the content of the lessons, they also do not adopt the social interactional rules for school literacy events. Print in isolation bears little authority in their world. The kinds of questions asked of reading books are unfamiliar. The children's abilities to metaphorically link two events or situations and to recreate scenes are not tapped in the school; in fact these abilities often cause difficulties because they enable children to see parallels teachers did not intend and indeed may not recognise until the children point them out.

and

> They seem not to know how to take meaning from reading; they do not observe the rules of linearity in writing, and their expression of themselves on paper is very limited.

Consequently, these children start off in school at a great disadvantage; their home environment, indeed their whole community, regards books, stories, writing and so on from such a different perspective and with such a diverse set of values that, unless they soon change their entire way of thinking and learning, they become very disenchanted with school and education and ultimately 'switch off' at a very early age. The children constantly find themselves being admonished either for their behaviour or for their lack of achievement. This community's record of 'school success' is obviously not very high.

Although not so different from mainstream children, the Roadville community children seemed, at first sight, to fit in with the school system much better than the Tracton children, but they also were seen to fail before the end of their primary years. These children, in contrast with the Tracton children, grew up surrounded by books and toys designed especially for them. Book reading was seen as a performance, but the children were not encouraged to compare anything they saw in the book to anything in real life (for example, the picture of the duck in the book bore no actual resemblance to 'real' ducks of their own experience, and they were never asked to compare the two). They were encouraged to fill in workbooks and sit still 'doing work'. At school, the Roadville children did very well at sitting still and listening, alphabet skills, colours, numbers, and answering 'What?' questions. They could not, however (unlike the Tracton children) comment about a story, talk about the motives of the characters, create their own stories or compare two stories. So, although they had mastered the 'social interactional rules for school', they were unable to think independently, create storylines, or think around any subjects. They initially seemed to do well in the early years at primary school, but by the 'fourth grade' (Year Four), where their ideas were beginning to be challenged and they were being asked to think for themselves rather than remember facts, they were already beginning to fail and also to become disenchanted and 'switched off' by school.

David Barton[9] has drawn on this research by Heath also to point out the mismatch between home and school practices. He says that children from the more middle-class, mainstream home will be more 'in tune' with the ways of the school compared with children from more working-class home environments; but even those most 'in tune' will find the practices of home and school very different from one another. Both Heath and Wells compared home experiences and environment with subsequent success in school. Wells, in particular, conducted a rare longitudinal study in which specific children were studied at home (pre-school) and then years later at school. He identified stories being read to the children as the 'most important variable linking the children's home and school achievement, more important than looking at books, drawing and colouring, or writing'.

Heath, however, as we have described, studied different minority cultures in the US to find out which kind of language use occurred, and how frequently the specific types of language use valued by schools occurred in various communities. She found that whatever the kind of community, its language and language use, it was the occurrence of specifically school-valued types of language use in the home which had any kind of bearing on subsequent school achievement or success. Thus different communities will produce children who are all 'in tune' to different degrees relative to the frequency of the types of school-valued language use at home. Children coming from different cultural environments will cope differently with the school and with the culture of books and learning to read. Some will find it very similar to home, and fit in straight away, while others will find it worlds apart from home and will find it difficult to fit in with the school's way of doing things.

One of the major problematic issues in the area of parental involvement concerns the question of whether the pedagogic practices of the school in a curriculum area such as reading can be productively imported into the context of the home, or whether indeed this is desirable. This question is explored in other chapters of this book, but is raised again here because home-school reading schemes have become very widespread in recent years. Gregory[10] argues that the practice of shared reading will take an essential part of its substance from the context it finds itself in, so that shared reading at home is an altogether different practice from shared reading at school. For her, a child's ability to interpret texts and to participate successfully in reading practices depends on the context. Children from low socio-economic backgrounds may well have wide experiences of literacy practices but these may be of a non-book nature[11]; so the assumption that 'shared reading with the teacher' will be commonly interpreted by all children cannot be made. Such children find it deeply problematic to position themselves in relation to reading practices contextualised by the school setting, and so attuning to the knowledge and discourse associated with this practice is not straightforward. They are like newcomers to a foreign society, aware of the strangeness of the cultural practices but not in a position to offend their hosts by critical observation.

We are reminded also by the French social theorist Bourdieu[12] that, in schools, children not only learn how to acquire language and literacy, but also learn a disposition towards language and literacy – that is to say, the social and institutional dynamics of the context provide a way of patterning relations to texts. As we know, in school 'real' books do not mean the same thing as 'scheme' books; and even 'real' books are not just books, they are perceived as tools for the teaching of reading. So the context in which children find books is crucial for determining the authority of particular kinds of texts and for determining the way readers and texts relate to each other. The way children make sense of texts, and the possibility of multiple readings that can derive from them, is co-produced by the agents and the context – that is: teachers, children and particular texts in school; parents, children, family and particular texts in the home; and children, peers and particular texts in the community. Some texts, like wrestling magazines, or horror and romantic 'teen' novels, will have considerable difficulty claiming currency in all contexts. Even a text that can inhabit a variety of these territories – perhaps a Roald Dahl favourite – will not mean the same thing in all of them. It will signify something quite distinct from context to context, because it is subject to a different interpretative community in each case.[13]

READING TELEVISION

'Welcome to Monster-Piece Theatre!' begins an episode of the popular children's television show *Sesame Street*. The Cookie Monster is standing in for Alistair Cooke to introduce 'Dances with Wolves'. This is not the Kevin Costner version, but one with a cute pink pig and a big bad purple wolf. A familiar theme with a predictable outcome, one might think. But not in this version. The wolf asks the pig to dance, and after several remonstrations of 'What big eyes you have, wolf!' (and so on) he eventually persuades her to join him, to rapturous applause from the couples of sheep, cows and other animals also on the dance floor. Of course, the wolf does not eat the pig, but discovers a new friend. This version of 'Dances with Wolves' draws on a variety of stories such as Little Red Riding Hood, the Three Little Pigs and other well-known traditional tales. It also peddles a moral theme, in this case something like 'We are all very different, but that doesn't mean we cannot live together.' All very moral and uplifting stuff, but what do young children make of such a medium and such a message?

Children who have been sharing books and stories, as well as television and video, with their parents and older members of the family since birth may be well-equipped to make sense of such a complicated inter-textual sketch. Without this history of sharing texts that draw on other texts for their vitality, not only would they miss the 'joke' of this version (as many of them undoubtedly did) but they would not have known what a story was in the first place. When we are confronted with a new medium and a new message (such as the one above), we know how to interpret it only by referring to other media and messages that we have experienced before.

This 'inter-textual decoding' requires no 'reading' in the traditional sense. All that was demanded was an understanding of what stories are and a superficial knowledge of the existence of traditional fairy tales. As the programme is screened for a pre-school audience, it is obviously assumed that children watching the programme have had such experiences – at home. So how does the home environment, before school and during the school years, affect how children learn to 'read' such 'texts', and what role do their parents have in mediating them?

Many researchers in media education and 'television literacy' argue that watching television is far from being a passive activity, at least mentally. Children's ability to understand the narrative logic of television drama, news reports, documentaries and even soap operas demands that the children are in an active dialogue with themselves.[14] (We refer again to this notion of a 'dialogic imagination' in Chapter 4.) The idea that, in watching television, children are in an active, albeit silent, dialogue with a 'social other' is borne out by the evidence of

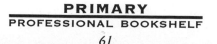

what children say about their own television viewing in recent empirical research done both in this country and other parts of the world.[15] Indeed, the reason why soap operas are so engaging for adults and for children is the very same reason why novels are so successful – they offer us the chance of being 'in' and 'out' of the action, of being engaged and being reflective, not just about the narrative action but about our own lives, experiences and culture (and our relationship to it). Children can learn about the nature of this process by watching *Neighbours* as much as by reading *Charlotte's Web* or *Eagle of the Ninth*. The diversity and depth of alternative readings may differ from one example to the next, but the nature of the process itself is evident in them all.

More than this, the mediation of any sign system depends on a social context to make sense of it and to verbalise it. This is one of the reasons why we include the viewing of television in a chapter on reading. There are a number of analogies that can be drawn between reading print and reading television; they are both visual forms of signifying meanings in continual transformational change which rely on socially-constructed understandings between those who 'produce' the images (the writers in particular) and those who 'consume' them (the audience or readers). The conventions and the codes of the narrative structure are not self-evident, but in both cases need to be learned. Because viewing television is almost exclusively a home-based practice, we want to attract the attention of teachers to the enormous possibilities and potential for learning that reside in developing critical 'readers' of the television medium.

As we have said, what it means to be literate depends on where you are, what you are doing and how literacy is defined at that time. As teachers we should be part of the way literacy is being redefined by the technological advances made in television, video, e-mail and the World Wide Web. We have a professional role to play to make explicit the knowledge about these media that, for children and parents, is often tacit, implicit and spontaneous.

One of the ways this can be done is to construct opportunities for children to talk about television in critical and self-reflective ways, both in school and at home. Contrary to the way it is often characterised, television viewing is for most children a highly social activity. For children and adults, it is usually done in the company of others, very often with family members. Even when it is done alone, viewers often talk back at the screen or will talk to others about what they have watched and, in doing so, construct views, understandings and standpoints. For children, this will often be done in a highly competitive atmosphere to gain status with their peers. Even adults, though they behave in more subtle ways, know that talking about television defines who we are.[16]

Discussions with parents about television viewing should not focus on how parents should select or regulate viewing at home. Indeed, this would only result in resistance and conflict. Parents will usually be keen to reassure teachers that they already regulate their children's viewing, just as they may tell you that they listen to them read regularly, never let them eat junk food and ensure that they are in bed early every night. Parenting, as many of you reading this will know, is ridden with guilt and feelings of inadequacy. Don't make parents feel worse by implying that their children are now watching too much television as well. Instead, point out that watching television as a social part of family life can be *good* for their children in lots of ways.[17] First, as we have said, it helps children make sense of all kinds of questions, issues and misunderstandings, and helps them to construct answers, opinions and knowledge. Discussing their likes and dislikes, favourite plot-lines and hated characters, guessing the endings to mystery dramas and playing along with gameshows is not only a pleasurable activity, but also helps them to become critical and self-reflective viewers. This kind of activity is not simply social, though that is a valid point in itself in the context of family life; it is also a development of communicative and cognitive competence in a socially constructed context which, as we know from Vygotsky, enables children to achieve more than they would be able to do if simply left on their own.[18]

Television can have a powerful motivating effect on reading. Teachers and parents can capitalise on the interest and enthusiasm of serialised children's novels on television. Publishers' sales soar at such times. Of course, there is an element of marketing manipulation involved; but that is true of all book sales, even to schools. One teacher we know used a televised Narnia chronicle to boost book sales at the school bookshop and then liaised with parents to persuade them to read the story aloud with their children at the same time that related activities were going on in class.

The Shared Writing Project (see Chapter 4 for further details) has included many writing activities that enable children and parents to reflect on their television viewing in positive and evaluative ways, such as focusing attention on and stimulating discussion about genres, categories, audiences, stereotypes, 'positive images', scheduling and keeping viewing diaries. The resources now available to teach media education at all levels of primary education are very impressive, and the use of them with children in class and with the involvement of parents can be a major fund of literacy and curriculum development. In our professional role as educators we can identify areas where children lack knowledge and understandings of the literacy of television, and create opportunities for them and their parents to develop those understandings in the place where television literacy, like print literacy, is initiated: the context of the home. Like the development of concepts in print literacy, television and other media literacies emerge from the dynamic interaction of spontaneous and reflective activity. The development of spontaneous concepts of television literacy have ample opportunity to develop in the social context of television watching in the home. Reflective activity, which is so important if children are to become independent and critical learners, is a function of instruction which makes the concepts of television literacy explicit and therefore subject to conscious deliberation and control.

THE DOMAIN OF THE SCHOOL

As opposed to the home environment, the school provides a fairly formal setting. There is a clear structure to each day that is generally dictated by the school – or teacher-imposed systems. The child quickly learns the rituals peculiar to school life: morning registers, putting your hand up before you speak, listening to instruction, knowing where the pencils are kept and where you put them at tidy-up time,

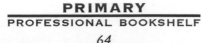

and so on. However close a teacher may feel he or she is to a class of children, the fact is that they are having to share their attention with thirty or so individuals, all with their own personalities and needs. The teacher cannot always be available to the individual child to the same extent that a parent can. Reading on a one-to-one basis may be confined to a short, time-tabled slot in the day. This may be as little as a few minutes a day; and some research suggests that even in well-organised classes, teachers were able to give their uninterrupted attention to children reading for no more than 30 seconds.[19] Teachers endeavour to give as much attention as they can to individual readers; but they cannot forget the rest of the class – always one ear or eye is on the others, and occasionally comments such as 'Quieter please', or 'Sam, sit still', 'Please don't fight over that book, that's how things get broken!...' and so on are needed to keep the peace, thus breaking the concentration and flow of whatever reading the child is doing. In this short time, teachers are listening, helping, sharing, enjoying and discussing the book with the child as they attempt to take note of the progress the child is making. Sometimes they manage to make a few notes, write in the child's reading diary and then tick them off the list. It does not leave much space for really 'getting into' a book and discussion, let alone any meaningful formative assessment or diagnosis of difficulty.

Schools vary greatly as to how 'formal' or 'progressive' their reading policy is; and though these are in many ways unhelpful terms which position teachers in an unnecessarily polarised debate, they are still used by many teachers as terms to characterise their own and their school's practice in this area. However, there do seem to be some views that are generally held by most teachers and schools; broadly, these are:

✦ 'real' books should be part of the reading curriculum
✦ reading 'scheme' books can be a good way of supporting development;
✦ the teaching of 'phonics' and spelling is an important part of learning to read;
✦ regular reading times (including 'quiet' and 'shared' reading) are important.

The variety of practices is of course enormous. Some schools now have a 'no scheme' approach, whereas others stick closely to a familiar reading scheme; others prefer to have a range of schemes available, alongside a rich variety of 'real' books. Books in the classroom will vary from school to school, especially in terms of the selection available for the children to take home. Some schools will have a wonderful selection of fiction and non-fiction, but will only allow reading 'scheme' books to go home; some will have a similar selection which the children can choose from alongside their reading 'scheme' books; others may have the odd book from a reading 'scheme' mixed in with other books, and the children have 'free choice' from the selection.

COMMUNICATION BETWEEN HOME AND SCHOOL ON THE TEACHING OF READING

So, given that there are inter-school differences in approaches to reading, what are the different ways in which we communicate with parents? Attitudes towards parents generally span from the 'Keep them at a playground's distance' motto to involving them at all opportunities in and out of school through parent meetings, fund-raising, parents in the classroom, use of a parent room, and so on. However, more schools are now making the effort to communicate with their parents regularly and qualitatively. Although as Roy Long points out in one study:

> Negative teacher attitudes and certain aspects of teacher
> professionalism and lack of confidence combine to produce
> parental compliance rather than parental involvement.[20]

So, instead of parents being valued within the school, he found teachers felt they needed to assert their roles as the professionals and keep the parents at a distance. Parents were found to be active in many parts of the school; but whether they had any voice, or were really listened to, was another question entirely.

In order to tease out some of the issues we have raised so far, we are going to look at three different school contexts and characterise their practices in short case study summaries.

CASE STUDY 1

One example of a school that has successfully and effectively involved parents in children's learning is a primary school in Banbury, Oxfordshire. Lesley, an Infants teacher at the school, describes it as having an 'Open door' policy in all areas. Parents are encouraged to share anything that they might be concerned about regarding their child with the staff, as this may affect the child's behaviour and ability to learn. Other factors, such as the charismatic headmaster and friendly school administrator, all contribute to a school that generally seems very accessible to parents. Parents are encouraged to be involved in school activities right from the start of their child's life there. At the initial meeting Lesley has with new parents, she makes a 'contract' with them, describing the kind of literacy and numeracy activities that she can guarantee will happen at school. However, she points out even this will not be enough for the children to achieve a certain level of literacy and numeracy by the time they leave the Infants; she tells them that their support at home through reading (PACT) and the shared maths scheme (IMPACT) is essential to their child's success at school.

> We feel that some of the responsibility is theirs (the parents'). You can't just say, as we did in the old days, that you learn to read and write in school, and you learn to play at home. Instead, they are interlinked and with all the goodwill in the world you can't hear every child reading every day, well not in the way we want to do it now, since the National Curriculum and probably before that. We say that we want them to be reading, not just barking out words. I say to parents that 'between us, your child will become a reader'.

The role of parents in their children's learning before, during and after school is clearly valued here. Parents are actively encouraged to help out at the school, and parent governors frequently visit and talk to the staff. Lesley considers her parent governors to be invaluable allies. They provide a bridge between worried or concerned parents

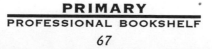

and staff. Parents who feel wary about approaching teachers about any concerns feel that they can talk to these parent governors. They might say things like 'Well, if you're worried that Johnny's had the same book for a week, go and have a word with Mrs Wright'; and sometimes they will even check with the teacher that these parents have been to see her, which then gives her an opportunity to ask them if everything is satisfactory.

> If they have a concern, I will always take it on board, because it is legitimate, even if it's one that you might have a laugh about in the staffroom later. To them, perhaps it's their first child, perhaps they are an anxious parent, perhaps they've found learning difficult themselves, and all of a sudden they might be thinking 'Gosh, if my child has the same problems as me it's going to reinforce all of those feelings that I had', or they might have an inkling that their child is not doing things as soon as other neighbourhood children.

Parents are listened to and taken seriously. Having said this, parents do not visibly affect policy: it is more a case of Lesley and all the other members of staff having an open line of communication there for every parent who wants to take it up. Individual needs are met, but all of this falls within the framework provided by a particular approach to the teaching of reading and a personal philosophy and understanding about how children come to be readers. However, Lesley herself has been personally influenced through being in contact with parents, and inevitably through experiencing parenthood herself. Like most professionals, she is constantly reviewing her own practice and ideas and has moved a long way from where she started out. When Lesley now goes on training days or courses, she tries to 'look at new ideas through the eyes of a parent as well as a teacher'.

For this school, the important feature of parental involvement in reading is the opportunity it creates for a dialogue to develop between teachers, like Lesley, and parents. Her view is clearly premised on what she calls 'a partnership' in educating children.

CASE STUDY 2

Schools which adopt a more 'progressive' approach to the teaching of reading, with reduced or no use of reading schemes, sometimes claim they have an uphill struggle communicating with parents who cannot identify with what is happening in the classroom at all. The more formalised an approach is, the more accessible it seems to be for parents, perhaps because it resembles the way in which many parents themselves learned to read. They may have experienced formalised reading schemes and flashcards, though probably school books were not generally taken home. The use of reading schemes appeared, then as now, to offer an easier and more manageable way to keep tabs on progression.

One example of a 'progressive' school that was studied is situated on a mixed estate of families from socio-economically advantaged through to fairly poor homes. Curriculum policies are explicit throughout the school and reading schemes are not used other than 'in special cases'. Word tins are 'definitely not used' and spelling lists and tests are a practice reserved for the juniors. Classrooms are brightly and neatly decorated, with a large selection of 'real' books attractively set out on bookshelves in each one. 'Scheme' books can be found in the school; but they are either treated as 'real' books, and mixed in with the other books, or used for 'extra support for children with reading problems'.

At this school, the concerned parents of one very able Year One girl attended some curriculum meetings on the teaching of reading. They asked a series of questions and, after the meeting, engaged in a long discussion during which the teaching staff failed to reassure them that the approach taken by the school would succeed in making their daughter a successful reader. Later, it became clear that the parents had invested in a home reading scheme and begun working through it at home. Within a few months the girl had learned to read.

This apparent confrontation between the school's approach and the wishes of the parents threw up a number of questions for the teachers and the school. Who and what was instrumental in the child learning to read? Does it matter what texts are used? Would she have learned anyway with such a high parental expectation? As far as the parents

were concerned, it was the reading scheme that finally 'did the trick'. For the teachers there were still some unresolved issues. What about other parents and their children? What do we do if all parents demand reading schemes? What are the other implications for the school?

This school has its approach to reading clearly and explicitly set out and considers it to be a professional matter. Staff make time to meet parents individually and chat about their children; in some cases, they even devise personal schemes of homework for parent and child to do together to supplement the normal classroom work. However, this school would not consider the option of actually changing any classroom practice because of a certain parent's wishes or even a group of parents' wishes. They are happy to adapt existing policy, for example by supporting struggling readers with games to take home and play, but the choice of using or not using particular approaches and texts was explained and justified to parents on professional grounds. Parents were given time and a forum to express their concerns and doubts, but the school was confident enough to stand by its professional judgements.

CASE STUDY 3

Another school in a similar setting to the previous example considers itself to be a mix of 'progressive' and 'traditional' methods. It uses a popular major reading scheme as its main reading scheme, supported by two others. Some teachers in the school send home word tins. The school has a relaxed and flexible attitude to the issue of continuity and progression through the various reading schemes, and teachers make adaptations for individuals. For example, in the class of one young teacher who describes herself as 'largely progressive' there is a full complement of 'real' books alongside the reading schemes, and she also sends home word tins with some of the children. This teacher remarked:

> At college, I would never have done this but then I thought 'Well, it's what some of the parents want, it might do some good, and it doesn't do any harm.'

This teacher was allowed the space to make this change by the school, since it has some members of staff already using word tins. Parents understand what an individual teacher's approach may be here, but they also know that as their child moves up the school this approach may change and that another teacher may take quite a different view. Here, parents know that they are listened to, and that the school is flexible and relaxed enough to let individual teachers take their views into account.

LISTENING TO PARENTS

In her widely read and influential book *Read with Me*, Liz Waterland talks about her model for communicating with parents:

> In every case where parents have successfully joined the teachers in reading initiatives the schools have worked very hard to contact and follow up as many parents as possible. They have also mentioned that there may be a point with a very few parents at which you have to accept that for whatever reason you are not going to win. This may be because the parents remain hostile to what you are trying to do. In which case they can either trust you or take their child to a school that will offer what they want...

She goes on to say

> ...parents cannot and should not dictate teaching methods (suppose each of the sixty parents of your class wanted you to do something different for their child?)

Schools have to decide what their approach is as regards the teaching of reading. It would be difficult to deny that at the end of the day this is a professional matter. Teachers are responsible legally and morally for deciding how best to teach children to read; but in deciding their approach, they should take parents into account. This means that schools need to consider several things:

✦ *Where do they want parents to fit into the process?*

For example, the 'contract' made by Lesley with the parents at her school guarantees a certain level of involvement right from the start: it is a 'partnership'.

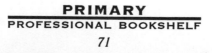

✦ *What are the lines of communication between home and school?*

Teachers need to explain what they are trying to do. Many issues, such as how they track progression in the children's reading, are confusing to parents and require explanation.

✦ *What happens if the approach does not seem to be working?*

If a child is struggling with the school's approach, then parents should be reassured that alternative strategies for the child are available.

TEN PRACTICAL SUGGESTIONS FOR INVOLVING PARENTS IN THE TEACHING AND LEARNING OF READING

Many teachers have understandably been apprehensive about involving parents because the issues surrounding methods and approaches to the teaching of reading have become highly contentious and politicised in recent years. Teachers who feel unsure themselves about the rationale of various approaches, or who may be inexperienced in rehearsing the rhetoric of the arguments, may well feel nervous facing searching questions about their policy and practice. This is very understandable, but teachers should not let it deter them from involving parents in reading. We have a professional responsibility to communicate with parents, and the onus is on us to do so by virtue of the authority that we carry as professionals. However, the following suggestions may be of help in preparing us to do this effectively.

1. Involve your colleagues

It is important that all members of staff are involved in discussions, especially those who say very little in staff meetings. It is vitally important that all the staff understand and support the scheme, even if you are initially concentrating on one end of the age range. Hopefully, with any home-school reading enterprise, you will eventually integrate the approach throughout even if it operates in different ways with children in different parts of the school.

2. Invite parents to help in the school

Inviting parents into the classroom to help with reading is also something that needs to be considered and planned carefully, particularly where the often integrated nature of literacy learning may need to be made explicit to 'the untrained eye'. Lay parents may not perceive the routines and structures that are implicit in many primary classrooms, and it may be wise to discuss these with parents beforehand in a specially-arranged forum, such as a preparatory meeting. Some of the pedagogic practices of the teacher in the classroom are 'invisible' to parents in the same way that some of the pedagogic practices of parents are 'invisible' to themselves in the context of the home (see Chapter 6 for more on this subject).

However, if parents are not already working with you in the classroom you may be missing out on a lot. Start off gradually and allow time for talking to parents, waiting for responses, asking for their assistance regularly, waiting for a few more to respond and so on, until it feels 'normal' to have parents in the classroom – in all kinds of roles. Try not to give parents the job of 'listening to readers' all the time – use them across the curriculum in the classroom. When planning the activities for the day, keep in mind who you have coming into the class and what you could give them to do. Make sure the parents who have volunteered understand the range of activities they may be asked to do. Put aside sufficient time either to explain the activity or to write clear instructions.

For example, parents in one school we know have the task of introducing new books to the group reading sessions in infant classes. By doing this, the teachers have enabled parents to realise that their contributions are their own and require some preparation on their part, which in turn results in a more active engagement by the parents. Too often parents are given tidying-up jobs which, though necessary, are hardly likely to inspire them to a regular commitment.

Get to know the parents that come in to help if you can. The better you know them and they know you, the easier it will be to communicate what you want them to achieve through an activity. Talk to them at the end of each session to get some feedback about how the activity went and how individual children got on with it. Make sure they feel valued. One nice way of doing this is to invite parents who have helped in the school to a lunch at the end of the year, so that they also feel a part of the school's social network.

Many teachers experienced in parental involvement feel that the strength of parents as educators is in the context of the home, where their intimacy and authority with their own children goes unquestioned and where the literacy practices engaged in are defined by the social processes of family life, such as the reading of instructions for a game or the writing and reading of a shopping list.

3. Visit the Home

Seeing children in their home environment can be very revealing. Observing their reactions to their parents at home and seeing how they react to other siblings is informative. What toys do they play with? Are there books or other reading materials? What do they like to watch on television? This is not an opportunity for you to snoop, nor (obviously) to comment on the home conditions. It can, however, be a wonderful opportunity for you to spend a little time with the children on their own territory. They can act as the host – they can show you their room, show you their favourite toy, or just sit and chat. Children remember these visits as very special times when they had you to themselves in their own environment.

Home visits are also a good opportunity to get to know parents, and provide an ideal chance to explain things like the school reading policy and the use of reading folders and diaries. Taking an example reading folder with you can be very helpful when explaining how it will be used with parents and children. Parents often ask questions about stages of learning and what is expected of them. They may ask questions about the reading scheme (or lack of one), or be worried that their child may struggle with the books in the class. It might be a good idea to take a few of the class books with you as examples in case the conversation goes in this direction.

4. Organise parent meetings and events on reading in the home

One way to get across your message about encouraging reading and writing that reflects the social contexts of the family and wider community is to stage a parents' evening where the emphasis is on practical involvement in authentic literacy practices and tasks. One school we have observed prepared for such an event by involving children in the painting and construction of 'props' and 'sets' that would make areas of the school hall resemble various rooms in the home. Room dividers and standing screens were covered with wallpaper and painted to create the settings of a lounge, a kitchen, a bathroom and a child's bedroom. Some items of furniture, such as easy chairs and sofas, were brought in from the staffroom and elsewhere to add authenticity to the appearance. It was emphasised that the nature of the evening was to be both practical and interactive, and parents and children were encouraged to move from 'room' to 'room' sharing a variety of reading (and writing) opportunities that might arise in the context of the home. For example, in 'the lounge' there were television listing magazines, and the children, with the help of their parents, were set the task of finding details about their favourite programmes. Another activity was to look through the holiday brochures provided and, as a family, choose a holiday that would suit given criteria for facilities, location and cost, then fill out a 'booking form' to reserve it. Many other similar activities were contrived to simulate such things as ordering merchandise from mail-order catalogues, reading and answering bills and invoices, reading and writing postcards and greetings cards to send to relatives and friends. The children were also encouraged to add their addresses to an address book that was provided. A diary and wall calendar were on hand to find and write in family birthdays. A Polaroid camera was available for children to take a family portrait, then make a frame card, write an accompanying caption and send it to a relative.

Teaching staff were on hand to orientate children and parents to activities that needed some guidance or explanation, and offer support should they identify situations where parents were reluctant or lacked confidence to participate. A member of staff positioned in the school office continually rang an extension phone situated in the 'lounge' while children were encouraged to answer it and, with the help of their parents, to write down a contrived message which they had to deliver and read to another member of staff. Word games were taught and played, lists made up of guests to imaginary parties, journeys planned and timetables consulted for trains and buses, notes of comparative prices for toys from catalogues were made, address books were compiled from telephone directories, and a wide variety of other reading and writing opportunities were contrived. Similarly, there was a range of other possible activities in the 'kitchen', 'bedroom' and, to a lesser extent (as one might expect), in the 'bathroom'.

5. Organise parent meetings and events on reading in the school

Unless parents are also teachers or come into school regularly, they probably have very little idea of how reading is taught in school or how they can help in the process. Meetings to explain approaches and methods can be an important part of communicating with parents and beginning the process of involvement. Organising a meeting requires a lot of time and effort and teachers want to see this rewarded, so preparation and planning are important. Letters sent home can be very impersonal, but are often necessary if personal contact is not possible with all the parents you want to reach. It might be useful to note here that letters written by, or decorated by, children are far more likely to be read by parents. Parents should be given plenty of warning before a meeting is to take place, and some idea of the purpose of the meeting should be outlined in the letter. A reminder should be sent nearer the time. Child care responsibilities and work patterns are extremely diverse these days, so a choice of meeting times is advisable. Try to make the school sound welcoming and the meeting interesting and relevant, so that you get at least one parent (or other adult) from each family attempting to come.

Some schools find it useful to invite an 'expert' to the meeting. This can help add credibility to your cause if you feel that parents are sceptical or even hostile to the approaches you are taking. However, do make sure that your 'expert' is an entertaining and persuasive communicator; there is nothing worse than a dull or uninspiring speaker – they will do more harm than good.

A SUGGESTED OUTLINE FOR ORGANISING A MEETING

Allow plenty of time to organise a meeting; you will need to think about writing letters, booking rooms, organising materials, making displays, and so on. You will probably need to start thinking about a meeting about a month or two before you expect to hold it.

a) Organise the space

Think about which room to use. If you have a small group of parents, using a classroom can be far 'warmer' than a large assembly hall. If you have a large number to cater for it is still better to keep the groups small, so try to arrange re-runs of the meeting on different nights so that all of the parents who are interested can attend.

Arrange the chairs in a circle or arc to allow the maximum visibility between speaker and parents. Try to make the atmosphere as relaxed and informal as possible. Remember, some parents may feel quite intimidated by just being in the school and may lack confidence of their own literacy.

Organise parents, or other members of staff, to be in charge of serving tea, coffee, wine or biscuits (it is quite a nice touch to have the teachers serving tea to the parents as this makes them feel much more like 'guests').

You might also want to display drawings the children have done in relation to reading and books (for example, 'I am sitting on Miss Edwards' lap reading' or 'I like books about pirates'), or posters for publishers and bookshops.

b) Plan the structure of the meeting

Welcoming the parents:

Ask your headteacher to open the evening, to welcome everyone, to introduce the speakers and to give a brief introduction.

Here are some suggestions for points to include in a 'talk':

◆ When children first come to school they already know a lot about writing and books. By the age of five the average child has learned to speak 2000–3000 words. Many children come to school already familiar with a selection of books and with some favourite characters.

◆ Most of what children know about language so far has been taught to them by their parents, who continue to teach their children throughout their lives, or at least until they leave home. We share the job of educating the children.

◆ 'Who can remember learning to read?' Many adults recall the 'pain' of learning to read when they were made to read texts that were too hard, or read bland texts over and over again. Some recall the pleasure of being taken to the library or having a bedtime story. (These are good starting-points for leading parents into discussions about making learning to read a pleasurable and satisfying experience.) What is the point of learning to read if, when you have done so, you hate it so much that you will never choose to read again?

◆ Not even 'reading experts' fully understand how children learn to read, and there is no 'one way' which works for all children. However, some strategies are more effective than others, and children need to be seen as individuals responding to a variety of strategies appropriate to their particular needs. Parents can be part of the process which identifies these different strategies. (You may want to explain that you aim to teach children not just to be able to read, but to become readers for life.)

✦ A practical activity that you may find useful involves asking 'How does it feel to be a struggling reader?'

Tell parents that they are going to be given a sheet of writing that has been deliberately made more difficult so that they might feel what it is like to struggle with reading. Hand out a sheet of clearly-typed mirror writing. (You can produce a sheet of mirror writing by photocopying a page from a newspaper article, or page from a novel, on to an overhead transparency sheet, then turning it over and photocopying it.)

Give them a few minutes to look at the task, and then ask if someone is willing to read it out. It is more difficult than it looks. Common mistakes include reversals like 'on' and 'no', having difficulties with short words, finding longer words easier to recognise, and generally finding it much easier to 'guess' words once they have an idea of the content of the writing. All of these are very similar to the kinds of problems early readers have with texts.

Once the activity is over, hopefully the parents will have an idea of what it feels like to be a struggling reader and the strategies used to deal with the difficulties. You can now start to explain why it is important to make the child feel relaxed and to make the occasion of sharing a book as pleasurable as possible. Next, explain how you teach reading in the classroom: reading with individual children, 'quiet reading' times, 'read aloud' sessions, group reading sessions, browsing and choosing, how you approach other reading activities such as cloze procedure, sequencing activities, sound and symbol matching and reading games. Parents may want to know how you keep track of who has read what and how they are doing. Be prepared to answer questions as you go, without getting sidetracked into issues that may not be of concern to all the parents.

✦ You may want to display the following points on a board or print them on a sheet or leaflet for the parents to take away:

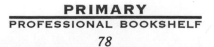

READING AT HOME: THINGS TO REMEMBER

- Read when the child wants.
- Sit somewhere cosy if possible.
- Let your child hold the book if he wants, and you be the one to turn the pages.
- Praise and encourage as much as possible.
- Talk about the whole book: the cover, the inside pages, the names of the authors and illustrators.
- Read the story to the child first, and talk about the pictures as you go.
- Discussing what is going on in the story and helping the child to develop responses is an important part of learning to read.
- Do not get stressed; this anxiety will easily be picked up by the child.
- Try to give all of your attention to the child; this is their special time.
- Stop when the child gets tired.
- Talk about the book, and relate it to things in the child's experience. (For example, if it is about a birthday party, talk about their own birthday parties.)
- Write a comment in the reading diary. (Have some examples of pages from a reading diary to show the kind of thing to write.)

6. Produce a booklet: 'Sharing Books with your Child'

Many schools which use a PACT-type shared reading approach also send home booklets. Generally speaking, schools write their own booklets which they can then update every few years. Frequently, this job is given to the schools language co-ordinator, and they do it on their own. However, it can be a very rewarding experience to involve parents in the task. Some schools in London have received grants from local arts and educational charities to do this. Arrange an open meeting to which parents are invited, and examine a range of booklets produced by other schools (Language Advisors in your area should be able to lend you some good examples). Read them through and talk about what the parents like about the presentation and content. How would they want it written? What information would they find useful? What size, format and design would they like?

In this way, you could go away from the meeting with most of the work done for you. Parents who opted to be involved will feel like they have had a say in something important, and will understand things much more clearly through having to talk about them and to make decisions about information included.

7. Set up Family Reading Workshops

Family reading workshops might be another strategy for developing parents' confidence with involvement in their children's reading. In some schools this has taken the form of discussions about the levels of difficulty of various books, the interest level and content, or various ways of talking about books and reading aloud. For such workshops to be successful, they need to focus on the concerns and interests of parents and to draw on their strengths rather than being conceived as a crash course in how to teach reading. Some schools we visit have established regular book making workshops where parents, many of whom have multilingual competence, have been encouraged to acquire book art skills and to share personal experiences or their various traditions of storytelling with the children.

Other schools have included ideas such as assembling a 'reading box' of favourite books, comics and magazines or a writing 'tool kit' comprising various pencils, pens, felt-tipped pens, a notepad, a notebook, scrap paper, stationery, a pencil sharpener, an eraser and a list of addresses for children to write to for free material. Many schools have also staged book-making evenings where stories have been told by parents themselves to provide the stimulus for parents and children to make simple concertina, zig-zag or stapled books together.

8. Set up a 'Family Literacy' Scheme

The Adult Literacy Basic Skills Unit (ALBSU) has produced a wide range of materials for parents to help their children with literacy. ALBSU also funds projects around the country, targeted particularly at parents who lack confidence in their own literacy, which bring together schools and local community colleges to involve parents in working alongside their own children in the classroom and in working separately on activities which develop their own skills. Much of the research on family literacy[21] suggests that promoting parents' confidence in their own literacy skills and practices is crucial to raising levels of competence, particularly in areas of high socio-economic deprivation.

9. Set up a 'Paired Reading' Programme

Other strategies, such as the introduction of paired reading schemes, have proved successful in various parts of the country.[22] This involves parents and children learning a phasing procedure whereby simultaneous reading is interlinked with independent reading. The process begins with the parent and child reading aloud together; and if the child omits a word or an error is made, the parent then allows the child time to provide the word. If she fails to do so, the parent provides the word, the child repeats it and they continue. Alternatively, if the child feels confident to take over from the joint reading she can produce a pre-arranged signal, such as a knock on the table, and the parent will remain silent until a mistake or an omission is made. The parent provides the word, which is repeated, and the reading continues simultaneously until the child indicates that she is ready to take over independently again.

10. Set up a Parent-run School Bookshop

For one school, the most successful way of involving parents in the development of reading was to set up a school bookshop, the running of which was later completely taken over by parents. Working in 'shifts' and rotas, a large group of parents took turns to order books, canvass the opinions of children, do the accounts and stock-taking, arrange displays and exhibitions and organise Book Weeks. Within a year they had made the bookshop a central feature of school life. School bookshops can create a forum where large numbers of children, parents and teachers gather and talk about everything from books to bullying. It can also provide an important opportunity for teachers to enquire about the reading preferences of children and parents, and to offer advice and recommend books that are being read in school. In this school, the phenomenal success of the school bookshop has been the major achievement of their parental involvement effort. By drawing large numbers of parents into the school informally, the teachers have broadened the communication links and improved the quality of the dialogue between parents and teachers. Not least in these days of financial stricture, it has also been a considerable benefit to the school fund.

KEEPING IT GOING

Inevitably there will be some parents who could not make it to any of the meetings, so 'reminder' letters are a good idea; or notes can be stuck into the reading diaries explaining such things as 'When, How and What to do' and 'What should I write in the diary?'

Refresher meetings remind parents what you are trying to do, and can catch any new parents of children who have started in the middle of a year. They also give parents the chance to evaluate the current scheme and to assess its effectiveness from their point of view. Such meetings can also allow parents to ask about developing issues; and as children learn to read, different questions will naturally arise.

Parental involvement in reading, in whatever form, is now so well established in schools across the country that it is inconceivable that we will ever return to a situation where parents will not be recognised and valued as an integral part of their children's literacy development. For some very innovatory schools, this foothold is the first step in opening up the school's policies and practices to the influences of the families and the community it serves; for others, it is the beginning of an exploration of how the resources of parents can be involved in enhancing other curriculum areas, as we shall see in the following chapters.

REFERENCES

1 For some interesting examples of networks of literacy see Moll, L.C. (ed.) (1990) and Hamilton *et al* (eds.) (1994).
2 Peter Hannon's book (1995) is the most recent and extensive research survey of parental involvement in literacy, and is drawn on substantially for this chapter.
3 Ivanic, R. and Hamilton, M. (1989) pp 15–17.
4 See Hilary Janks' materials on Critical Literacy published by Hodder & Stoughton, for practical ideas and activities on developing critical attitudes to literacy.
5 Hannon, P. (1995) *op.cit.* p 39.
6 See the fascinating ethnographies of pre-school literacy in Wells (1987) and Tizard and Hughes (1984).
7 French, H. J. (1989) 'Listening to children read: an analysis of teachers' responses', unpublished MA thesis cited in Hannon (1995).

8 Heath, S.B. (1983).

9 Barton, D. (1994).

10 Gregory, E. (1992) 'Learning Codes and Contexts: a psychosemiotic approach to beginning reading in school' in Kimberley, K. *et al* (Eds.) (1992).

11 See the work of Taylor and Dorsey-Gaines (1988) for fascinating examples of non-book literate 'survival' practices in a New York urban district.

12 Bourdieu, P. (1977) cited in Buckingham, D. (1993).

13 See Fish, S. (1980).

14 Buckingham, D. (1993) pp 27–28.

15 For interesting accounts of empirical research on young children and television, see also Messenger Davies, M. (1989) and Hodge, B. and Tripp, D. (1986).

16 Buckingham, D. (1993) pp 39–40.

17 Maire Messenger Davies (1989) has written a research-based but entertaining argument about how television is 'good' for kids.

18 Buckingham, D. (1993) p 177.

19 Taverner, D. (1990) p 13.

20 Long, R. (1993) 'Parental involvement or parental compliance? Parents' role in school improvement', in Merttens, R. *et al* (Eds.) (1993).

21 See Taylor, D. (1983); Taylor, D. and Dorsey-Gaines, C. (1988) and Teale, W. H. (1986).

22 For an explanation and report see Topping, K. and Wolfendale, S. (1985).

PARENTAL INVOLVEMENT IN MATHS

Mathematicians are like Frenchmen: whatever you say,
they translate it into their own language and henceforth it is
something completely different.

Goethe

Parental participation, as we have seen, always raises a number of
issues concerning the boundaries of the teaching profession. How is
the expertise of the teacher constituted? In what sense can a parent
be considered an expert? What are the effects on respective status of
the differences in expertise, and how do these constrain productive
dialogue? In this chapter, these issues take on a new dimension which
has to do with the subject matter – mathematics.

WHAT IS MATHS?

Many teachers report that this is one of the most difficult questions they
are asked; and nine times out of ten, it is the children who ask it. Most
parents, and teachers, take it for granted that we know what maths is,
though they would be hard-put to define it. The dictionary definition of
mathematics talks of a 'science of number and magnitude and all their
relations', and the word itself has its provenance in the Greek words for
'skill' and 'knowledge' and is related to the root of the verb 'to learn'
(*mathema*). A famous story refers to the difficulty. A physicist working at
Los Alamos after World War II was having difficulty with a particularly
intransigent problem. Seeking help, he went to the great Hungarian
mathematician John von Neumann, who was at Los Alamos as a
consultant. 'Simple,' said von Neumann, 'This can be solved using the
method of characteristics.' After the explanation the physicist said, 'I'm
afraid I don't understand the method of characteristics.' 'Young man,'
replied the mathematician, 'In mathematics you don't understand things,
you just get used to them.'

Whether mathematicians understand their own subject or not, they are almost universally perceived as being very clever. Maths is always thought of as a 'difficult' subject – as opposed to the humanities (English, history and so on), which are perceived as being much more comprehensible. It is also significant that mathematics forms the basis of almost all intelligence tests. Despite the fact that the whole notion of 'intelligence' as an innate property of individuals has taken something of a battering in recent times, nevertheless the idea persists that mathematics can somehow be construed as 'pure reasoning', and is therefore a guide to those who are 'clever' rather than 'just' knowledgeable or skilled. In this respect, maths has taken over from Latin as being the subject which we teach because it teaches children 'how to think'.

Another way of looking at the academic reputation of mathematics and mathematicians is provided by a joke told by Ian Stewart in his book on modern maths. An astronomer, a physicist and a mathematician were holidaying in Scotland. Glancing from the train window, they observed a black sheep standing alone in the middle of a field. 'How interesting,' observed the astronomer, 'All Scottish sheep are black.' 'No, no,' the physicist responded, 'Some Scottish sheep are black!' The mathematician sighed deeply and then corrected them. 'In Scotland, there exists at least one field containing at least one sheep, *at least one side of which is black.*'

The definitions of maths most often reproduced in connection with primary education concern three aspects of the subject:

✦ generalisation and abstraction
✦ relations, connections, patterns and functions
✦ communication using systems of signs and symbols.

Paradoxically, none of these refers directly to number or arithmetic – which are almost certainly the two topics mentioned by parents when they are asked what mathematics consists of, and which are the two aspects which receive most teacher time in terms of classwork.

At one time, many educationalists appeared to rely heavily upon an almost Platonic concept of maths. There was, so to speak, a large bag labelled 'Maths'; and theoretically at least, we could say what was inside it and what was not. Thus many arguments raged around the question of whether a specific topic or fact was or was not *really* maths. Much of the debate surrounding the documentation produced by the Schools' Council, the Nuffield Foundation and other curriculum groups concerned the contested nature of what could be counted as 'maths'. Currently, we witness a move towards a consensus that maths, like science, may be regarded as a social construct. In this sense, there is no such thing as 'real maths': there is simply a consensus at any one time as to what is and is not 'mathematical'. Maths, on this view, becomes one domain amongst others within the area of social practice, defined, as are other domains, by reference to its terminology, vocabularies, rhetorics, rituals, routines and activities.

The National Curriculum does not define mathematics as such. It does not even define mathematical terminology or 'correct' mathematical vocabularies. However, it does talk about developing 'mathematical language' and provides a list of skills, concepts and knowledge. Most teachers take this list as being fairly definitive, expecting it to provide the parameters for their practice in teaching maths as well as to create a general understanding of 'what maths is'. There has been some criticism regarding the cultural bias of the list, and also its derivation from the needs of a particular socio-economic class. However, there are few arguments in teaching nowadays which rely upon a notion of 'true maths' in the sense outlined above.

PARENTS AND MATHS

Parents are frequently insecure in relation to maths. Unlike illiteracy, a degree of innumeracy is publicly acceptable: 'Me, I can't add two and two and make four!' People will commonly refer to disliking maths, and newspapers use the term maths as a byword for boredom. There is some evidence that women are more likely than men to feel inadequate in relation to their own mathematical competence and also, by derivation, in terms of their ability to help their children in this subject. Thus a mother who reads on a daily basis with her children and who helps them learn to write will quite often avoid maths on the basis that 'I'm no good at that, I'd probably do more harm than good.'

There are two consequences of this widespread dislike and fear of maths on the part of parents and other care-givers. The first relates to the issue of professionalism. In the area of maths, most parents perceive the teacher as the expert. Because they perceive their own mathematical knowledge as lacking, the teacher is construed as the one who 'knows'. Clearly this is not always the case. Some parents are both knowledgeable about and confident in mathematics. But in a significant majority of cases, in relation to maths (unlike writing or reading) the teacher's expertise is construed in terms of *subject* rather than *pedagogical* knowledge. Thus the teacher 'knows maths', whereas she knows 'how to teach' reading or writing. The parent, in the majority of cases, knows what reading and writing are, what these skills consist in – whereas they do not feel themselves to possess this knowledge in relation to maths.

The second consequence relates to the very real possibility that teachers may reinforce disadvantage in this area. A child at secondary school comes home with some maths homework. He can't do it, and his Mum hasn't a clue! The mother very likely failed maths the first time round. Now, she feels herself to be failing a second time round – only it matters more this time, because it is someone she loves who may suffer. For some children, this is not a problem. Either they have parents who can help them, or their mother says, 'Don't worry, dear, I'll get you a maths tutor.' But for many parents, this situation is precisely their worst fear realised. They feel themselves to be 'disabling' their own children – something they are most anxious to avoid in relation to their children's education.

TEACHERS AND MATHS

Many teachers are less happy with the maths curriculum than with either reading or writing. Some of the factors mentioned earlier apply to teachers as much as to parents. Fewer primary teachers took maths at university than took any other core subject. Many primary teachers do not feel either confident in or inspired by maths as a subject. The nature and quality of the teaching of maths which many teachers themselves experienced at school probably did not supply a model for their own practice. In addition, we have witnessed three major sets of change to the content and the approach of the National Curriculum for maths in six years, and teachers feel both annoyed and confused by these changes.

DOMINANT RHETORICS

A rhetoric may be defined as *a way of saying things*: an informal structure of phraseologies and vocabularies, tones and terminologies. The dominant rhetorics in a domain both prescribe and proscribe what can and cannot be said at any one time, and how it may and may not be expressed. They constrain and afford our descriptions of the subject itself, and of entities and events within the subject. They enable us to discuss and debate, to describe what happens, to express ourselves, and to construct biographies of others in the context of this subject. There are several rhetorics in maths education, some of which have enjoyed a brief period of prominence and others of which have been around for almost a decade. Phrases and terms which evoke these rhetorics include:

✦ the maths of everyday life
✦ maths as a problem-solving tool
✦ multicultural maths
✦ maths investigations
✦ calculator-assisted learning
✦ practical maths.

Depending upon the audience, some or all of these phrases or their associated vocabularies can be found in almost any piece of documentation in maths education. Some teachers refer to the 'buzzwords' without whose presence any whole-school policy, course introduction or preface to materials would be deemed lacking. However, despite a vocabulary of apparent consensus, it is far from clear that the rhetoric translates comfortably into a set of classroom practices or even into a shared set of meanings. Some teachers have reported an increasing sense of confusion within maths education. Ten years ago, the name of the game was Cockcroft[1] – practical was in, rote learning was out, investigation was in, routine practice was out, problem-solving was in, repetition was out, and so on. If teachers were interested in promotion, if they attended courses, the orthodoxy was evident and well-known.

Currently, however, the situation is far from clear. There is a perceived push towards what used to be called 'basic' numerical skills. The presence of tests – including what is effectively an 11+ – has raised the profile of written computation. Although children working from textbooks is only regarded as 'good practice' if it takes place within very defined limits, none the less commercially-produced maths schemes are once again on the agenda. The notion of the teacher as an instructor rather than someone who simply 'facilitates mathematical learning' is no longer to be discounted.

Teachers therefore find themselves in a difficult position. The tests produce their own pressures, and there seems to be a general consensus that post-Cockcroft maths education had swung too far in a (so-called) 'progressive' direction. Parents prefer sums, is the general belief – however, this is not substantiated by some of the research. Inspectors and advisers are looking for quality of teaching in maths as in all the other subjects, and the National Curriculum has foregrounded number and numeracy at the expense of some of the other mathematical areas. The purpose of some of the initiatives and the ways of framing things which were popular in the '80s is no longer clear, and their value is contested. Teachers as well as parents are looking for ways of helping children to cope with tests in maths, as well as the demands of a broad curriculum.

PARENTAL PARTICIPATION IN MATHS

Given the situation in flux described above, we might think that involving parents in the maths curriculum at the moment is the last thing we need to do. As one headteacher said to an advisor who was talking to her about launching the IMPACT project in her school, 'Well, I would, but quite honestly we need to get our maths curriculum sorted out at the moment. When we've done that, we can then think about involving the parents.' The advisor replied that he was quite happy for her to keep the parents out while they sorted out the maths in the school, *provided that they kept the children out too*. Since we have no option on the latter, we may as well accept that if the children are involved then, inevitably, the parents are too.

THE IMPACT PROJECT

The most thoroughgoing and successful attempt to involve parents in children's learning of maths has been the IMPACT project.[2] This initiative dates back to 1986, when six schools in North London piloted a system of using shared homework activities to encourage a greater

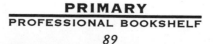

level of parental participation in their children's maths learning. The basic idea behind IMPACT paralleled the development of the PACT project in reading (see Chapter 2), and relied upon the use of take-home shared maths activities. A crucial part of the system, however, was the mechanism supplied by the IMPACT diary which accompanies the activities, and through which a dialogue may be set up and sustained between parents and teachers. The whole IMPACT process can be formulated as shown in Figure 1.

It is easiest to describe IMPACT in practice through a couple of examples.

1. A teacher was planning the arithmetic for the week with her six- to seven-year-olds. She decided to send home an activity which required the children to make rubbings of one of each of the coins of the realm along the top of the page. Under each coin, they then had to draw or stick something that they could buy using only that coin. Thus, under the rubbing of the 10p, they might stick one-third of a Mars bar wrapper. This proved to be quite a difficult activity, since the children and their helpers had to be quite inventive to think of something costing just 1p! However, they rose to the occasion magnificently, and evidence of creative and lateral thinking was easy to see. One child had stuck a small amount of bird seed on her page, and her Mother had written: 'This is the amount of bird seed that Ben the Budgie eats for exactly 1p!' Another had stuck one-third of a slice of bread, having calculated that this was the amount of bread we get for 1p, and lots of the children had stuck the wrapper from a 'penny chew'.

When the children all brought their pieces of paper back into the classroom, the teacher had them work in groups of four or five. They calculated the amount of money you would have to spend in order to buy all the edible things on their sheets. They worked out the amount each sheet was worth in all, and discussed how much you would have if you not only had one of each possible coin, but also had one of each possible banknote. The whole class participated in a discussion about the value of each coin and the sorts of things you could buy with each one. Finally, the children did an exercise in their maths books calculating the amount collected if you have ten of each coin. The teacher then made a display of all the children's homework sheets along the entrance hall of the school.

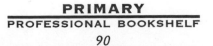

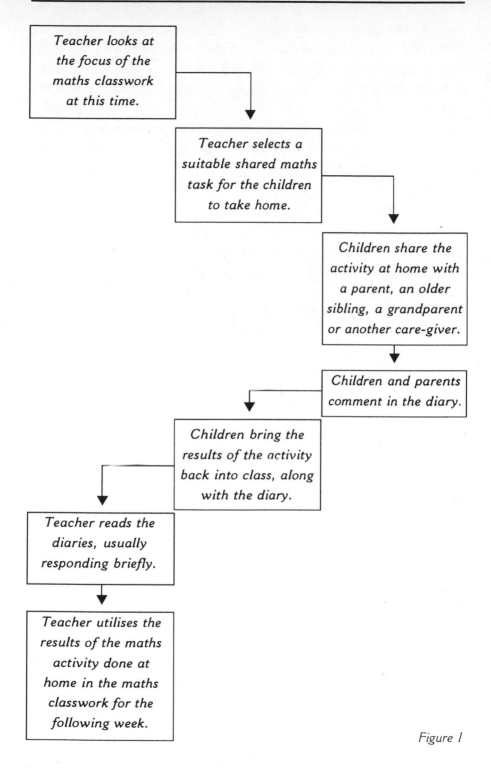

Teacher looks at the focus of the maths classwork at this time.

Teacher selects a suitable shared maths task for the children to take home.

Children share the activity at home with a parent, an older sibling, a grandparent or another care-giver.

Children and parents comment in the diary.

Children bring the results of the activity back into class, along with the diary.

Teacher reads the diaries, usually responding briefly.

Teacher utilises the results of the maths activity done at home in the maths classwork for the following week.

Figure 1

The parents and the children reported having enjoyed the activity. Some parents commented that it surprised them that their children did not in fact recognise all the coins without help, and one parent said that he thought this was because nowadays children do not 'run down the shop' on their own. They may accompany their parents on the once-a-week shopping expedition to the local supermarket, where all the items are marked with bar codes rather than prices; but this does not help them to recognise coins, especially since many parents will pay with cheques. The parent added that this meant it was very important that both parents and teachers helped children to familiarise themselves with 'real' money in a shopping context, since they might not have these experiences 'naturally'.

2. A reception class teacher had sent home the following IMPACT activity:

---

*IMPACT: SHARED MATHS
HOMEWORK*

*Ask a grown-up to help you!
They must lie down on the floor!
How many spoons long are they?
Find as many spoons as you can. Lay them
alongside their body, starting at their feet
and ending at their head.
What do you do if you run out of spoons?
Write the number of spoons long the helper
was, together with their name. Draw a
picture of your helper.
Bring your work into school.*

When the children all brought their pictures and numbers into school, they discussed the numbers of spoons — what the largest number and what the smallest number were. They drew out their numbers with coloured crayons and pinned them on a line in order. They were then encouraged to fill in the gaps, writing in the numbers which had not been drawn. They also each coloured in a pre-drawn spoon, wrote the name of their helper on it and stuck it on the graph above the number representing their helper's length in spoons. They then discussed which lengths occurred most frequently, who was the longest and who was the shortest.

One thing which made them all laugh happened when one of the children said that she couldn't find enough spoons and so she used forks. She said she had then run out of forks as well and so she had used a corkscrew. She drew forks and a corkscrew beside her spoon for the graph. Another child claimed that the 'helper' had been the cat – and he was five spoons long with his tail stretched out! The whole class discussed what else you could have done if you didn't have enough spoons. Several children explained that they had used one spoon repeatedly. Some had, as above, used things that were the same length as spoons, such as forks. The teacher used the opportunity afforded by this discussion to introduce the idea of a repeated and constant unit of measurement.

The shared maths activity which is sent home to all the children each week is accompanied, as shown in Figure 1, by an IMPACT diary. This is a small book in which parents and children are encouraged to comment on how the activity went. Each activity has a line-up in the diary like the one shown in Figure 2.

	PARENT		CHILD		
Name of Activity	**Was IMPACT enjoyable?**	**Was it too hard?**	**Did you like your IMPACT?**	**How much did you learn?**	**Comments**
	Great fun ☐ All Right ☐ Not much fun ☐	Too hard ☐ Too easy ☐ Just right ☐	a lot / a little / not much	a lot / a little / not much	
	Great fun ☐ All Right ☐ Not much fun ☐	Too hard ☐ Too easy ☐ Just right ☐	a lot / a little / not much	a lot / a little / not much	
	Great fun ☐ All Right ☐ Not much fun ☐	Too hard ☐ Too easy ☐ Just right ☐	a lot / a little / not much	a lot / a little / not much	
	Great fun ☐ All Right ☐ Not much fun ☐	Too hard ☐ Too easy ☐ Just right ☐	a lot / a little / not much	a lot / a little / not much	

Figure 2

The parents' and children's comments in these diaries are extremely illuminating. They have been the subject of a research project reported elsewhere,[3] and provide an indication of the parents' interest and readiness to be involved in their children's learning at the 'local' level of the acquisition of particular skills. Through the diary, a mechanism is supplied whereby parents can make assessments of their children in relation to clearly-specified mathematical skills. The diaries also provide a means of setting up and sustaining an efficient dialogue between parents and teachers over a prolonged period of time. This dialogue results in a greatly improved discussion in the annual or bi-annual parent-teacher interviews where the child's progress is reported on and discussed. From being a passive recipient of information about the mathematical progress of the child, the parent becomes a partner in a conversation in which both partners are contributing to the child's summative assessment. 'He seems to be improving in his understanding of numbers above ten', comments the teacher. 'Yes, he got on much better with that "Snakes and Ladders" game we had for IMPACT last week. He could write nearly all the numbers up to thirty-six,' the parent responds. This type of discussion exemplifies the extent to which what was traditionally a teacher monologue has been transformed into a dialogue.

DIFFERENCES BETWEEN IMPACT AND PACT

We can observe several differences between this process and the shared reading (PACT) on which it was originally modelled.

✦ There is (almost always) something material in the IMPACT work which comes back into class. The fact of a material object, such as the picture of Mum being measured with spoons, or the paper with the coin rubbings and slices of bread, coming into class makes a great deal of difference. It means that the parent's and child's work in the context of the home is recontextualised as 'classroom' maths (which does not happen with the reading work). It also allows the possibility, in theory at least, that activities which are generated in the context of the home can permeate the classroom context. One Indian mother came into class to show the teacher how a maths game that had been sent home with the children was very similar to a (rather better) game that she had used to play in India as a child, using pebbles. The whole class then played the new game and related the maths it involved to the more formalised classwork in their maths books.

✦ A crucial step in the IMPACT process involves the teacher explaining the activity before the children take it home. Therefore, the person who knows what is to be done is the child — who must, in turn, explain the activity to the task-naive adult. This means that any translation necessary can be done by the child. This translation may involve a change of language, as when a child from a Bengali household translates the IMPACT activity into their home language so that they can share it together. However, even when the languages of the home and the school are both English, there will still be an element of translation. The child will have to translate a piece of classroom maths — what has to be done and why — into the vocabulary and terminology of the home.

The task is, as was mentioned above, unashamedly a piece of 'school-mathematics', notwithstanding the fact that it may well draw upon or employ the resources of the home for its successful completion. The child is well-versed in this 'school-mathematics'. The parent is, inevitably, naive in this respect. The regulation and articulation of the task as it is elaborated in the context of the home will pass back and forth between child and parent. Throughout the negotiation of the task and the generation and construction of possible, probable and imagined solutions, there will be a sensitivity on the part of both participants to those aspects of the task in which the other is inexpert — 'Miss said we had to...' and 'When you draw that line, hold the ruler further along...'

✦ In the course of sharing a maths activity together, parents and children will have to negotiate the meaning of the actual mathematics involved. When sharing a reading book, both parents and children are familiar, roughly speaking, with what the activity looks like. They know what 'reading' is, and they are more likely to have a shared sense of the process in which they are engaged. The same cannot be said of the maths. If a child comes home with an IMPACT activity which requires that he and his Mum make a graph together, the very idea of what a graph looks like, its construction and presentation, may have to be

negotiated step-by-step. It is likely that the final outcome will emerge as a product of this negotiated activity, and that neither party has a clear and distinct idea of what the result will look like in advance.

The IMPACT project has now been running nearly ten years, and has expanded from its original six schools in North London to be the largest programme of its kind in Europe and North America. In all, over 6000 schools in Britain are participating, and there are now six regions in the USA and Canada that have launched IMPACT. The idea that homework can be transformed in this way – from a way of rehearsing more classroom-based activities to a means by which the parents become involved in the process – is now firmly on the agenda.

COMBATING SOCIAL DISADVANTAGE

As was stated earlier, homework is implicated in the processes by which social divisions are reinforced and sustained through the institution of schooling. A parent who failed at maths, and whose memories of maths at school are characterised by boredom and bewilderment, is not in a good position to help a child struggling with interminable pages of maths homework. By contrast, the parent who understands – and even enjoys – the subject is able not only to assist and support her child's learning, but also often to share her enthusiasm in such a way as to generate the same in the child.

We now have evidence that involving parents through a shared homework scheme proves extremely effective both in raising the standards of children's achievement and in empowering those parents and children traditionally most marginalised by the schooling process. This evidence emerged as a result of a particular government-funded programme, the Haringey IMPACT Project,[4] which was designed to raise achievement in inner-city schools. The programme involved eight schools in the borough of Tottenham, in North-East London, all located in an area of extreme social and economic disadvantage.

The findings from this particular project support the view, based on previous long-term research on IMPACT,[5] that most children have an adult carer who is very keen to support their learning, and who, given the necessary help, will provide weekly assistance with a task. These carers need to be reassured that their help is valued and productive.

From the outset on IMPACT, it was clear that the numbers of children and families participating was a crucial factor. An early and surprising finding on the project was that the response rate was not related to the social class of the catchment area of the school;[6] in terms of the numbers of parents and children doing their IMPACT activities, a school in Newham or in Redbridge could get just as good results as a school in Oxfordshire. We discovered fairly early on that the single biggest factor affecting the number of children actually completing an IMPACT activity was the enthusiasm of the teacher,[7] though the number of parents actually commenting in the diaries did appear to be related to the social class of the catchment area. Two interesting addenda to these findings concern the fact that the response rates for IMPACT are often higher than they are for the shared reading – more parents share the weekly maths activity than participate in PACT – and the importance of the age of the children. Only 62% of Y5 and Y6 children participate in IMPACT, as opposed to over 85% of younger pupils and 96% of nursery and reception children.

The Haringey Project bore out these results. In almost every class there was a core of children who completed their IMPACT activities fairly regularly, some who were haphazard and a few who never managed to complete the tasks. As one teacher graphically put it, 'At the beginning of each term, I have three piles of IMPACT diaries – one pile, the largest, is those children who do IMPACT sometimes; a second, smaller, pile is those who do IMPACT every week. The third, very small, pile is those who almost never do their IMPACT. During the course of the year I aim to shunt all the diaries into the second set. It is true that I do manage to shift most from the first set into the second, but I don't touch those in the third set.'

However, a means of touching those in the third set was available. We noticed that the response rate was variable, with some teachers achieving a 100% response and others in which 60–85% came back. Since the teachers were self-selected and all of them were enthusiastic, the variation in the numbers of children/parents participating could not really be explained by the 'teacher-enthusiasm' factor. The main difference appeared to be the extent to which IMPACT could be said to be voluntary or compulsory. In exploring this, the teachers focused an

issue which is often implicit in debate about parental involvement in children's learning, but is rarely made explicit.

Two of the teachers, both of whom got response rates of 100%, had decided to make IMPACT virtually compulsory. They had achieved this by the strength of their expectation that it should be done. As one teacher put it, 'I tell the children that I expect them to find someone who will share their IMPACT activity once a week. I say that they can find either a grown-up or an older child, a brother or sister, a granny, an auntie, a friend, that it doesn't have to be a parent. I explain that they have to find someone, they can't do it alone; that it will be fun, that they will enjoy it and that it will really help their maths. I give them three weeks at the beginning of term to sort it out, then I tell them that they have a choice. They can either find someone to share their IMPACT with at home over the weekend or, at the latest, on Monday evening, or they can stay in at lunch-time play on Tuesday and do it with me. I say that I will be pleased to share it with them, that I shall enjoy doing so and it will be nice for me. But I point out that Tuesdays are football playtimes. They all sort it out to find someone to share it with at home.'

When other teachers in the group raised their concern that an approach like this put undue pressure on the children, especially those who did not get much support from home, she responded: 'But those children, the ones who don't get support, the ones whose parents tend not to read with them or come in to see the teacher, those children are precisely the ones who will not do their homework at secondary school, and will gradually "drop out" or "turn off" because no-one is giving them support. This is the pattern we have to break. If we don't break it now, they will do just as we all expect. And they *do* find someone to share their IMPACT. And they enjoy it. And now some of the Mums are coming in to see me.'

The question of whether this was a justifiable strategy occupied much of the group discussion time. Most teachers opted for a middle road – suggesting that they expected IMPACT to be done, and being prepared to 'chivvy' the children but not to 'force' them. For the project researchers, it raised a real dilemma. The teacher quoted above was right: the home is the single biggest factor in children's educational success. The children whose parents never read with them, do not share the IMPACT activities and do not come into school and attend the parent interviews are those most likely to be the homework casualties in the lower secondary school and the truants later on. They are least likely to get to university or college. She *did* break this pattern. The children *did* all find someone to help them; and in some cases at least, this proved a turning-point for both the child and the helper. It is possible (even likely) that support, once established, may continue into the crucial next stage of their education.

We should stress that the teachers were almost unanimous in their conviction that the children enjoyed doing the IMPACT activities. Despite the fact that not all children were bringing their IMPACT back into school, the attitude of the whole class was (nearly always) overwhelmingly positive. Many teachers felt that the children's ability to 'think mathematically' had increased substantially over the year. Teachers and parents all commented that the benefits to the children's understanding of number were clear. Children practised their tables, number bonds and other routine skills in a fun way, 'without making the process a chore'. As one mother put it, 'By the time my daughter had finished the IMPACT activity, she knew all her five times table.'

The findings from this project suggest that shared homework materially improves the chances of traditionally 'disadvantaged' children succeeding at school. The question is then whether we are justified in making such homework 'compulsory' for young children (those in Years 1 through 4). We know that parents are, on the whole, doing maths at home with their children, but that often both the pedagogy and the content may conflict with 'school' maths. Shared mathematics activities such as those provided by programmes like IMPACT would appear to provide a means of bridging this gap. But the question remains: what support can we offer those few children for whom no home assistance is forthcoming? As Rousseau put it, 'A child who is unloved is ineducable.'

OTHER WAYS OF INVOLVING PARENTS IN MATHS

Many schools have found other ways to open up the maths curriculum to parents. Some of these augment and complement a programme of shared maths homework such as IMPACT. We can categorise them under three headings:

1. MATHS EVENINGS

Many schools like to hold curriculum evenings when parents are invited to look at a selection of the maths resources and a talk is given about the school's approach to teaching maths. This talk is sometimes given by the maths co-ordinator within the school. On other occasions it is an invited speaker, such as a local maths inspector or advisor, who speaks to the parents, occasionally on a specific topic such as the use of calculators.

These evenings can turn out to be disappointing, with only a handful of parents – usually those who don't really 'need' the talk – turning up. It is fairly common to hear teachers complain that the parents they would really like to be there don't come, and that the parents aren't really interested. The experience of many schools would suggest that the best way to get parents to come into the school is not to refer to the maths curriculum! Research and practice both indicate that the majority of parents are not interested in the maths curriculum *per se*. But they are very interested in their own children's progress – or lack of it – in mathematics. Therefore, the most successful events build on this interest. 'Come and find out what your child is doing in maths, how we teach it, how they learn it...' is the general line of approach. Putting out a variety of maths games, puzzles and activities, as well as a selection of the books and worksheets that the children use, is an essential next step.

The format trialled and used in many of the schools who piloted the work of IMPACT up and down the country may be summarised as follows:

✦ *Parents come in; tea/coffee/wine/cheese/biscuits etc.*
A warm welcome!

✦ *Short talk about maths in the school – the general approach and methods used.*

> ✦ *Some joint maths activities. Parents working with the person sitting next to them or in very small groups. (See examples below.)*

> ✦ *General wander round – parents going to look at a variety of 'stalls' on which are set out different maths activities for them to try.*

The 'shared maths' part, when the parents do some activities in pairs and then feed back into the larger group, is the aspect of the evening which really seems to bring about a sense of belonging to a learning community. Many parents have commented that they saw and understood a great deal of how the maths was both taught and learned during this session.

Examples of the type of activity used in step 3 are shown in Figure 3. There are other activities suitable for group sessions in the IMPACT books, especially 'What a trick!' or 'A problem of age!' in the KS2 Algebra book.

2. 'HELP YOUR CHILD WITH MATHS' SESSIONS

These sessions can be held during the day, after school or in the early evening. They do not need to be very long – between half an hour and one hour is the norm. In some schools, teachers give these sessions themselves; other schools work in collaboration with the local adult education centre or college. Typically, these sessions are held in a classroom or parent room in the school, wherever parents feel most comfortable. If they are being run after school or in the early evening by teachers, there is often a video provided in an adjoining room for the children of those parents who wish to attend. If they are being run by local adult education centre staff, they are frequently held in a room large enough to accommodate a few toddlers or babies and some toys.

The sessions vary in nature and content, but most take parents through both the philosophy behind the ways in which their children are being taught maths and the content of the maths curriculum itself.

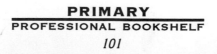

Guess the number

You need two people to play!

One of you thinks of a number between 1 and 99. They do not say it out loud.

The other person must guess what number it is.

BUT – they can only ask six questions – and the answers can only be 'yes' or 'no'.

So I might ask, "Is the number bigger than 50?" or " Is the number even?" or "Does it have a '3' in it?"

Can you guess the number in six questions?

Now you think of a number and let the other person have a turn at guessing.

They can only have six questions as well.

Figure 3

Story-time maths

Listen to this story!

Once upon a time there was a boy called Fred. One day, his uncle gave him 40p to buy a comic. Fred was very pleased. He bought his comic and went and sat in his room to read it. His brother admired it, so Fred told him he could have it for 50p. His brother paid the 50p and took away the comic. But then, Fred's uncle wanted to see what Fred had bought with the 40p. So Fred went and asked his brother for the comic back. But his brother made him buy it back for 60p! Fred took his comic and went outside. The kid next door was there, and Fred managed to sell him the comic for 70p. Fred went in and told his Mum the whole story. " I'm very happy," he said. "I've made money on the deal." Fred's mum laughed. "You are an idiot, Fred. You haven't made a penny!"

Who's right, Fred or his Mum? And why?

Thus a school in an inner-city area in the North of England held seven sessions of half an hour each at 3.30pm every Thursday. The course programme ran as shown in Figure 4.

It is not always this grand; some schools run only one or two sessions and combine several of the above, or touch on a much more limited area of maths. The attendance can be excellent for this type of session, and many schools have found that they serve a whole range of purposes.

Some parents come because they want to help their children and they are worried that their own maths is too weak. The sessions can sometimes provide more or less covert help for parents' own mathematical skills under the guise of showing parents how we teach children those skills. Thus if the teacher is explaining how we teach subtraction, she will inevitably be explaining how to do subtraction. This is why the adult education service is usually very interested in working in partnership with schools on what is effectively an adult numeracy programme.

3. MATHS TRAILS OR GAMES

These can be an occasional, but very powerful, means of helping parents to get involved in their children's learning of mathematics. Once again, practice varies here from school to school. Some schools put aside a session once a month – for instance, in the hall on the first Tuesday of the month – to have a 'maths games' afternoon which runs for about an hour up until school ending time. Parents who wish to are invited to come early, with their little ones if they like, and sit and play maths games with their own and other people's children. Normally, these sessions rotate and each class has a turn, but sometimes it is just one or two year groups which are involved. These afternoons provide a wonderful and informal chance for parents to come and share some maths with their children. Many of the conversations which take place over the Snakes and Ladders board are invaluable in terms of the information they impart or the trouble they save. A parent who is having a bit of a problem with some aspect of the maths curriculum in relation to her child's learning may welcome the chance to chat about it 'naturally' and in a relaxed manner while attending this sort of maths afternoon.

Help your child with maths!

Week 1.   *Counting to one million and beyond!*
           How children learn to count; how we help them
           to read, write and order the numbers.
Week 2.   *Adding up and taking away.*
           How we teach addition and subtraction.
           Games you can play which practise these skills.
Week 3.   *Multiplication.*
           Learning our tables; which ones first?
           How parents can help.
Week 4.   *Division.*
           How we teach it. How we make it make sense!
           Activities which can help.
Week 5.   *Telling the time.*
           When should they be able to do this?
           Digital and analogue. How do we teach them?
Week 6.   *Measuring.*
           Which units? What do they all mean?
           Come and find out, and then you can help them!
Week 7.   *Shape and space.*
           What they have to know.
           How we teach them.

Figure 4

CONCLUSIONS

Teachers – and parents – often suggest that maths is the most difficult area of the curriculum in which to build a productive partnership between home and school. Parents are nervous of the subject, and often claim not to know any maths. Teachers feel pressurised, and may not be able to define either the subject itself or its related pedagogy.

However, we have found that, contrary to what we all believed would happen, parents and teachers can work in partnership extremely productively in this area of the curriculum. The shared maths homework

schemes have demonstrated beyond any shadow of doubt that most parents can and will share maths activities on a regular basis with their children if given the chance. Furthermore, if this does happen, not only does the children's mathematics improve, but the chances are that those children most likely to be marginalised by traditional homework are less likely to experience such problems here.

REFERENCES

1 *The Cockcroft Report*, (1982), HMSO.

2 Merttens, R. and Vass, J. (1990) *Sharing Maths Cultures* Falmer Press. Merttens, R. and Vass, J. (1993) *Partnerships in Maths: Parents and Schools* Falmer Press.

3 Merttens, R. and Woods, P. (1994) *Parental Involvement in Children's Assessment*, AERA.

4 'The Report to The DFE on the Haringey IMPACT Project' 1994, published by UNL Press.

5 Merttens, R. and Vass, J. (1990), ibid.

6 Merttens, R. and Vass, J. (1990), ibid.

7 Merttens, R. and Vass, J. (1988) 'Raising Achievement or Raising Standards?', in *Education* 3–13, Vol 13; II.

PARENTAL INVOLVEMENT IN WRITING

> Writing is a complex cultural activity... [it] must be relevant to life... [and] should be cultivated rather than imposed. Children should be taught written language, not just the writing of letters.
>
> *L. S. Vygotsky*

THE TEACHING AND LEARNING OF WRITING

One of the greatest problems teachers face in relation to the teaching of writing is trying to convince children that it's worth the effort. Any single reason that a canny teacher can come up with to persuade a child to write something down will be countered by at least a dozen reasons why it would be easier simply to say it. Perhaps this explains why there have been comparatively few initiatives to involve parents in the development of their children's writing and why, even to this day, it is an uncharted territory in terms both of intervention and research. Perhaps, as Michael Stubbs[1] explains, spoken language has 'superiority' over writing in many areas: it existed long before writing was invented, is acquired 'naturally', has more social functions and is a universal attribute of human culture. Children probably sense this, but they also sense that writing is socially more important and has more status.

The rationale for writing something down rather than saying it is not obvious to adults, let alone young children; but that is not to say that children don't enjoy 'making their mark' on the world even from a very young age. Lev Vygotsky, a Russian psychologist working in the 1930s, observed that even babies are making the beginnings of spatio-symbolic representations by gesturing with their fingers and hands,

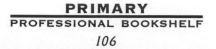

which he characterised as a kind of drawing in space. When children learn to hold the tools of mark-making, such as crayons and pencils, they are learning that the gestures they made with their fingers and hands can now become fixed concrete 'objects' on paper. Though their marks may be scribbles, children are learning that these marks are observable and can be added to and changed.

They go on to learn that they can recreate and represent observable objects from their surroundings by drawing their pets, their toys, themselves or their parents, or that they can create objects of fantasy which can be a source of dramatic play and be invested with a dynamic life of their own.[2] They learn that objects can come to denote other things, so they can pick up a fork at the dinner table and use it to play 'dive-bombers' on their food. This move from the concrete real object to the concrete symbolic one is crucial in learning about writing, because it is only when children know that one object can be a *symbol* for another that they can come to know that words written on paper can be symbols for speech.

The emphasis in the discussion so far has been on the child learning rather than the child being taught. We will redress the balance somewhat in the remainder of this chapter; but it is fair to say that the greater part (by far) of research into children's early writing indicates that children are making discoveries[3] and learning through a process of *enculturation*[4] rather than responding to direct instruction. As children mature, of course, their ability to be instructed develops. They learn *how to learn at home* and they learn *how to learn at school*. They learn language, the chief tool of instruction, to regulate what they need to know. Try teaching a child something they can already do, and see what reaction you get! They learn and practise other physical and mental skills too. The dynamic process of self-regulated instruction, discovery and practice develops a learner's capacity to be instructed further. The ability to be the subject of self-regulated instruction is, it is generally understood, a defining feature of what it means to be human.

Children's representations or drawings of objects in their surroundings tell us a great deal about their intellectual and emotional development; but they also tell us whether the children are beginning to understand the difference between *representing* an object by drawing its physical features as shown overleaf:

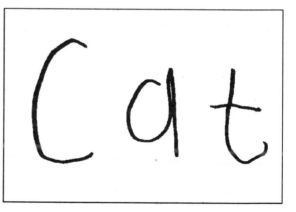

and *symbolising* an object by drawing its name, that is, writing it in this way:

Observing the development and evolution of children's drawing and writing behaviour can provide us with evidence about whether they have made the cognitive shift to knowing that they can not only draw *objects*, but they can also draw *speech*.[5]

In this crucial sense, then, writing can be said to be 'drawing speech'; and it is when children realise that this is possible that they have begun to understand the function of written language – or in linguistic terms, the concept of the *sign*.

The notion of the sign was introduced into the study of language earlier this century by the Swiss 'father of linguistics', Ferdinand de Saussure. As we have said in Chapter 2, Saussure proposed that the basic unit of analysis in linguistics, the sign, is made up of two elements: form and meaning. The form, which he called the *signifier*, is equivalent to the letters, words or images which refer to any given concept of meaning. For example, the letters *c-a-t* above (and the drawing, which I will return to in a moment) refer to a concept, that of a real cat. The meaning, which Saussure called the *signified*, is equivalent to the real object: the furry four-legged animal that has whiskers and miaows. Saussure claimed that the relationship between the form (signifier) and the meaning (signified) is arbitrary, as demonstrated by the fact that every language has a different form for referring to the same meaning; for example, the Italian *gatto*, the Russian *koshka*, the Punjabi *billi*. However, the drawing of the cat (as a 'form/signifier') is not arbitrarily related to the concept of the real cat ('meaning/signified'): it has a relationship to it which is motivated by presenting aspects of its physical features.[6] The letters c, a, t do not represent aspects of the physical features of a cat; as we have said, we could use the letters k, o, s, h, k, a and still mean the same thing. But in using the letters c, a, t we are using writing; that is, we are drawing *the speech* that comes out of our mouths. We even use a metaphor of speech to explain it; as teachers we might ask, 'What does it say?' and children might answer, 'It says cat'. Of course, letters and words written or printed on paper don't *say* anything: we make them *speak*.

The difficulty for teachers in all of this is that when asked, many young children drawing a picture will tell you not just what the picture *is* but what the picture *says*. Some will draw a picture of a cat and say, '*This is my cat. His name is Rusty.*' Others might say '*Rusty is chasing a mouse.*' One is a description of the drawing; the other is relating what the drawing *says*, as though it were writing. The crucial point here is not that the child cannot distinguish between a drawing and a piece of writing: she may well be able to do so. The point is that she may not yet understand that a drawing does not 'say' the same thing to anyone who might 'read' it in the way that writing does.

Drawing a picture involves encoding meanings which cannot be decoded in the same way that writing can. Writing can be decoded (at least in literal terms) by everyone who knows the code.

Putting this another way, the child has not yet *abstracted* from the drawing to understand that writing is a system of marks which symbolise speech. (Some would say it symbolises meaning, but that is another story!) They may understand that both drawing and writing stand for something beyond these processes, but they do not yet realise that writing stands for speech. They have not 'got' the sign concept in relation to written language.[7] Of course, there is an historical precedent for this which goes back to the earliest cave paintings of human civilisation. Such pre-literate behaviour should be viewed, not as evidence of arrested development, but as reassuring evidence of the uniquely human urge to symbolise our intellect. 'At the basis of all writing stands the picture.'[8]

MEDIATING PRACTICES IN THE HOME

A number of studies have shown that many children have developed this concept of the sign — that is, knowing the difference between what drawings represent and what writing says — before they enter school. Ferreiro and Teborovsky (1982), in what is now thought to be a classic study of children acquiring literacy before school, described the variety of spontaneous literacy events pre-school children experience in the context of the home. This and other studies[9] provide considerable evidence that an understanding of the sign, perhaps the most crucial of all conceptual acquisitions, emerges in the domain of the home. The role played by parents, therefore, in the mediation of signs is critical. But what is the nature of the mediating practices that parents are involved in? Furthermore, how does this mediation take place in the home? We can explore this with an example.

One of the authors was visiting friends. The five and a half-year-old boy of the family, Benjie, was playing a game which he had made himself. He asked the author to play. It was a counting game written on a large piece of scrap paper. The trail of numerals up to 18, some reversed, were randomly placed along what resembled a winding track. Benjie had cut a circular piece of paper as a counter. Looking at the

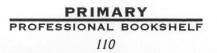

apparently random nature of the game, the author declined the invitation on the grounds that he did not know how to play it. 'That's OK,' said Benjie, 'I've written some instructions.' (See Figure 1.)

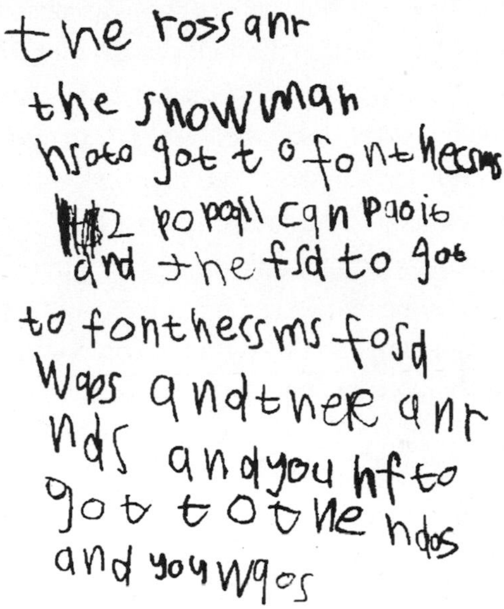

the ross anr
the snowman
hs got t o fon the crms
2 po pqil cqn paoi6
and the fsd to go6
to fonthecrms fosd
Waos and tner anr
nds andyou hf to
go6 t o6 Ne ndos
and you w9os

Figure 1

the rules are
the snowman
has to get to father christmas
2 people can play
and the first to get
to father christmas first
wins. and there are
numbers and you have to
get to the numbers
and you win

Benjie   age 5.6

He read them and then demonstrated how to play. His mother later explained that though she sometimes played board games with him, she was often too busy and encouraged him to make and play his own games.

The process of teaching the game was *tacit* – that is to say, Benjie had not been specifically taught the game by his mother; but as with the teaching and learning of any game, he was enculturated into the practice of it by playing it. His mother's strategy of encouraging him to make and play his own games is not just the survival strategy of a busy mother coping with domestic duties, but the strategy of all 'teachers' in relation to learners: 'I've shown you what you can do with the tools, now go ahead and use them.' This strategy creates for the child an opportunity to make sense of the game – that is, to make discoveries about number and writing, to play with sequence, to devise a set of instructions and to write them down so that by making them explicit to others, he is making them explicit to himself. Later, he finds someone to practice the game on – and in turn, takes on the role of instructor himself. The issues relating to the tacit pedagogies of the home will be explored in more detail in the final chapter.

EXPLAINING INVENTED SPELLINGS

One of the most striking features of Benjie's writing shown above is his use of 'invented' spellings. His writing is not copied, traced or imitated, though clearly there is evidence that he is drawing on the genre of writing rules he may have encountered many times when board game instructions have been read aloud to him. In this case, he is generating writing, using words that have become part of his inventory of known words and letters that he has included because they are intended to represent sounds. This kind of writing is often characterised as 'emergent writing', because it arises from activities that reflect real purposes for writing. Thus literacy emerges from social practice.

There are various stages of invented spellings.[10] The first stage is often referred to as the pre-phonemic stage. This is where children are imitating aspects of written language that they have seen, and they want to demonstrate that they can do it too and are part of a 'literacy club' that knows how to communicate through symbols.

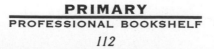

This may take the form of 'pretend writing' – that is to say, scribbles – or letter-like shapes that children will often be able to 'read', clearly expecting the writing to have a message.

Figure 2 shows an example of pre-phonemic writing.

I went to my sister's house

Maria   *Age 4.10*   *Figure 2*

The second stage is known as the semi-phonemic stage, where children begin to use letter names to represent words. Figure 3 shows an example of a child at this stage.

This example shows that the child has begun to understand and use sound-symbol relationships. This stage is often characterised by the absence of vowels. The generative, that is to say productive, nature of children's discoveries about writing is again underlined by the historical precedent set by other languages, such as Hebrew and Arabic, which evolved without

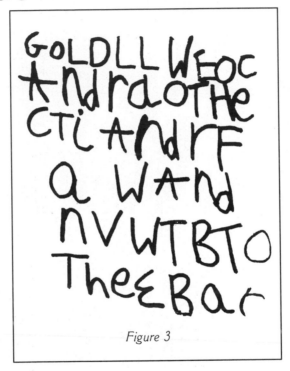

Figure 3

> *Goldilocks woke*
> *and ran out the*
> *cottage and ran far*
> *away and*
> *never went back to*
> *the 3 bears*
>
> *Maria*   *age 6.1*

the use of vowels in the writing script; and even today, vowels are used as additional symbols only for those learning these languages. The Greek civilisation inserted vowel symbols into script, and invented the 'alpha-bet'.

A third stage in the development of children's invented spellings is known as the phonetic stage, where children begin to demonstrate a more complete knowledge of sound-to-symbol relationships and include more letters, particularly vowels, in their writing. Figure 4 shows an example of this.

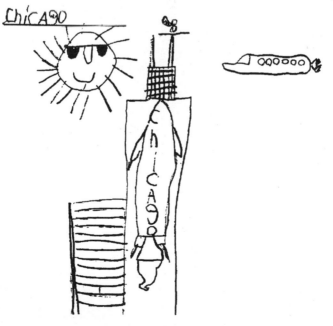

Figure 4

> *Chicago*
> *The tallest building in the*
> *world, it's called the Sears Tower.*
> *It has 110 storeys high*
> *I'm not talking the biggest*
> *building in London we're talking*
> *the biggest building in the*
> *world and I went up it*
> *You can see the whole of*
> *Chicago*
> *Matthew*   *age 5.9*

There is a fourth stage, commonly referred to as the transitional stage, when it is clear that children are beginning to draw on reading and other literate experiences to inform and expand their growing inventory of spellings. In the final stage, most of their spellings are conventional and they are able to draw on a variety of visual and mnemonic strategies to achieve regular close approximations.

It is important to explain the logic of invented spellings to parents, so that they too can encourage and promote the exercise of this habit in their children's home-based literacy practices. Young children invent new words when they are learning to talk, often to the amusement and satisfaction of adults. Inventing spellings as a strategy in learning to write is, to them, a logical extension of this. Some parents, like some teachers, need to be reassured that validating invented spellings is not encouraging poor spelling. This is not a difficult task, but it can be a time-consuming one.

A parents' meeting which demonstrates the writing approaches taken in school can be an effective and important vehicle for explaining such issues and offering the reassurance that is sometimes needed. It would be a mistake to assume that parents will automatically be sceptical of or hostile towards encouraging developmental writing or invented spellings in their children. It would also be a mistake to use such meetings as a forum to convert parents to an outlook which supports the approaches of the school. Often parents are simply unaware of or confused about approaches, and value consultation and explanation. The result of this can be better information for the teachers and school, and a validation of the tacit, almost invisible instruction that parents produce regularly for their children. After one such meeting where one of the authors had been invited to speak, a parent wrote:

> I had never even imagined that there were stages in learning to write before you got into a classroom and a teacher showed you how to form letters.

WRITTEN LANGUAGE OR WRITING?

Here, one could draw a useful distinction between the 'compositional' aspects of writing and the 'transcriptional' aspects of it.[11] On the one hand, that part of the writing process which focuses on the assembling of ideas and the construction of the grammar, *the creative aspect* (what Vygotsky called 'written language'); and on the other, that part which focuses on presentation, layout, handwriting or typing and spelling, *the secretarial aspect* (what Vygotsky called 'writing'). Frank Smith argues that trying to deal with both parts of the writing process at the same time causes one to interfere with the other, and that even professional writers cannot deal equally with the demands each makes. The preoccupation with one always, however marginally, leads it to take precedence over the other.

Many teachers incorporate this view into the strategies they use to teach writing, by reassuring children at the beginning of a writing session:

> 'Don't worry about spellings or making your work look neat...'
> 'Concentrate on your good ideas at this stage...'
> 'When you've finished and you're happy with what you've written... you can write it up neatly... or make it into a book.'

By making children aware that writing is not one unitary process but two processes, and by separating these and focusing on one aspect at a

time, they not only enable children to set achievable goals for themselves but are also likely to improve the quality and quantity of children's efforts.

Making various aspects of the writing process explicit is just one of the ways that teachers can help children to become more accomplished writers. The National Curriculum for English (1995) states that children

> should be taught to use:
> ✦ compositional skills – developing ideas and communicating meaning to a reader, using a wide-ranging vocabulary and an effective style, organising and structuring sentences grammatically and whole texts coherently;
> ✦ presentational skills – accurate punctuation, correct spelling and legible handwriting;
> ✦ a widening variety of forms for different purposes.

The National Curriculum document helpfully makes explicit the range of writing opportunities that should be made available to children at Key Stages One and Two. It refers to:
✦ the *purposes* for writing (such as writing to narrate, inform, instruct, greet, complain, enquire, gossip, persuade, describe, thank, recount, protest, enquire, reflect, explain, invite, and so on);
✦ the *forms* of writing (such as letters, lists, posters, playscripts, notes, poems, diaries, obituaries, novels, signs, lyrics, leaflets, brochures, recipes, reports, comic strips, and so on);
✦ the *audiences* for writing (such as peers, parents, teachers, themselves, the class, the school assembly, public bodies, private companies, public figures, publishers, imaginary people, relatives, historical figures, famous people, and so on).

Making explicit the purposes, forms and audiences shows written language to have the potential to be a functional, meaningful and rewarding activity. If children are going to be confident and competent users of literacy, they will need to have a real sense of it as a social practice that can be marshalled and harnessed to serve their purposes. They will need to build up a store of satisfying experiences where they have known written language to be useful for exploring and expressing personal feelings, perhaps across gaps of time and space, to

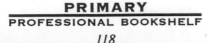

people they may never have met; where they have used written language to contemplate and think more clearly; and where they have realised that they can not only store and retrieve information using written language, but can also come to know that same knowledge better as a result.

In the last two decades, teachers' perceptions of the nature and processes of children's writing have changed drastically. Although Vygotsky (among others) wrote about this issue in the 1930s with a clarity that now seems amazing, it has taken many years for the insights drawn from his psychological research to influence teaching practice. Even until relatively recently, it was widely assumed that children learned to write only after receiving formal instruction from teachers in schools. Though he traced the pre-history of written language and its progression through gesture, play, drawings and scribbles, Vygotsky stressed that learning to write was an 'artificial skill' which was learned in school. Even now, many teachers feel unable to identify and draw on the linguistic resources that young children bring with them to school, and find it difficult to develop independence in their young apprentice writers. Tracing over letters or copying underneath the teacher's writing is still a widespread practice which as many teachers have recognised, can be both time-consuming and inefficient. It often results in numbers of children with their hands in the air waiting patiently (or not!) for the teacher to come and help them write something, or a line of children waiting by the teacher's table to write down a caption on their picture. From the point of view of teaching writing it is not the most effective method, as it wastes the opportunities for children to use their own knowledge and resources creatively – that is, to discover concepts about writing for themselves and to learn from their mistakes. It binds the child to an unhealthy dependence which is frustrating for both the child and the teacher.

What has been difficult for many of us who made the painful shift from this model of teaching writing was redefining our role as teachers of writing in what has come to be known as the 'developmental model'. For some colleagues, the removal of what seemed to be visible structures for the teaching of writing were inadequately replaced by seemingly invisible guidelines for the *learning* of it. Some teachers found

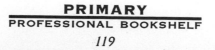

this a frustrating and confusing experience. Some children, as a result, were neither given instruction nor guided to make discoveries.

A MODEL FOR PRACTICE

Teachers need to have a framework in mind which defines their role in the process before they can effectively help children to learn about writing. Whatever framework they adopt needs to be understood sufficiently for them to be able to explain it. One framework which we have found very useful in articulating theoretical approaches to learning in parental involvement has been the *Teach, Make Sense, Practise* model of classroom education discussed in the Introduction (see page 11 and below).

Within this model, the teacher is sometimes a provider of facilities which allow this activity to go on. For example, children need resources to write: an adequate and well-maintained stock of papers, pens and

---

TEACH

✦ Teachers actively instruct, narrate, model and explain.

MAKE SENSE

✦ Children make this knowledge their own, and make sense of what they have been taught through a variety of means, including stories, practical activities, problem-solving tasks, games, puzzles and investigative, exploratory and creative work.

PRACTISE

✦ Skills often require practice and reinforcement. This can be achieved through activities on an individual basis, in pairs and in small groups.

---

other writing materials. They also need other resources to support them, such as dictionaries and picture dictionaries, word books and thesauruses, friezes, wall displays, writing corners, typewriters and word processors. In other words, they require an environment which not only facilitates but also promotes literacy. The teacher must also observe the children's progress, in order to intervene when help is needed. They need to ask themselves whether the children need:

✦ more whole-class modelling of story beginnings;

✦ more narrating of story structures;

✦ more small-group shared writing where some children will have more opportunity for direct input;

✦ more time to make sense of writing by making discoveries and mistakes for themselves;

✦ different resources;

✦ different writing tasks.

MODELLING WRITING

One of the methods by which teachers can create and model a variety of writing purposes and forms is through shared writing workshops and activities. With young children who are not yet confident and independent in writing, this may take the form of the teacher modelling the writing. This could be done with a group of five or six children sitting around a table while the teacher scribes on a sheet large enough for all to see, or even with the whole class sitting on the carpet area while the teacher scribes on a large sheet clipped to an easel. Many teachers have learned to use these sessions for effective mediation of concepts and skills crucial to the development of writing. One Reception Class teacher we have worked with recently started such a session by announcing to the children seated on the carpet that, as it was Monday morning, it was time for writing the 'Weekend News'. She asked the children what they had done over the weekend, and skilfully connected her own anecdotes with those of the children. Quickly, she moved the activity on and asked the children to discuss with each other, in small groups of two or three, what they had enjoyed doing over the weekend. Immediately, the children turned to

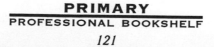

each other and began talking – a practice that had become a well-established routine over two terms as the precursor to writing.

After about two or three minutes, she interrupted and asked the children not to tell their own accounts, but to relate to the class what their partners had told them. This was not just a skilful teacher tactic for making sure they listened to each other, it also situated the child in the position of 'the other' – that is, telling a story in a way that was procedurally unlike the telling of his own. He had to *objectify* the characters and events to himself and others by becoming his partner; whereas when he told his own story, he was subjectified within his own narrative and could assume the perception of his listeners to be his own. (In other words, his listeners could 'see' what he was 'seeing'.) Having to tell someone else's story helps children to begin the process of *disembedding* their thought. Now that they cannot assume their listeners know what they know, they become what Margaret Meek calls 'the teller and the told'. This is an essential prerequisite to the acquisition of literacy.

The teacher then allowed a few minutes for children to share their partners' stories with the whole class, occasionally asking questions for clarification but more often responding with laughter or an empathic comment. The children, however, aware that the context of this talk was related to what was about to follow, could clearly be heard attempting to shift the structure of their oral speech towards conventions that they knew to be appropriate for written language. They were assembling, drafting and sorting ideas into shape and order. They were literally rehearsing in speech what they were about to compose in writing. They were beginning to talk (as far as they could at five years old) like writing. Often, teachers model this assembling or brainstorming of ideas on a sheet of paper.

After taking three or four contributions from the children, the teacher turned to the easel positioned next to her and flipped through the sheets of paper clipped to it, on which were written some previous days' news items. 'Whose news have we had lately? Oh, that's Gemma's news. Remember that, when she was sick in the playground? And that's Salvador's news when he went on holiday...' and so on, turning the sheets and reviewing what they had written in

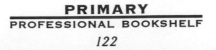

previous days and weeks. She and the children formed a consensus about whose news was the most interesting that day. Later, she told me she had engineered that consensus because there were children in the class who had not yet had their news written about. She began to write a child's news as she had been told it, which reflected the child's growing awareness of the conventions of written language. The mediating directions and the questions she asked the children showed that she was teaching specific points about the conventions of writing which arose from the range of experience and ability in the class. She differentiated the ability needs by directing the attention of individual children to specific teaching points:

> Now if we write 'Robbie's News', does anyone know what we put in between 'Robbie' and the 's' in 'Robbie's'?
>
> Now what do we leave in between the words as we write? That's right, a little space... you can put your finger there if you like, so you don't write in it... you do that next time, Siobhan, because you're apt to forget that little space – aren't you love?
>
> What sound do you think comes at the beginning of 'went'? *(looking directly at Jason)* That's right Jason, now what letter do you think makes that sound? ... Not a 'y' but that is a very good guess – and you'd think it would be a 'y', wouldn't you, by the way 'y' sounds? English is a funny old language, isn't it? Have another guess. . . yes, that's it. . . good lad *(writing it on the sheet)*.

For the next ten minutes, she was 'modelling' writing to all the children; and while maintaining a pace that kept the engagement of all or nearly all of the children, she was also teaching specific points about the conventions of the composition and transcription of written language. Every so often there was a rereading, as a whole-class recital, of what they had written.

After about ten minutes, three sentences were completed and the teacher asked the children to move off to their respective activities around the room. Two of the six groups in the class (about ten to twelve children altogether) would write their news in their own 'News Books'. These children would now have the opportunity to try to make sense of writing, and to make their writing make sense. They would have the freedom to make mistakes and discoveries by trying it out for themselves and asking questions, knowing that the teacher's support was close at hand and that she was sympathetic to their approximations and efforts. Some of the writing produced would still be of a shared nature, because some children would still be dependent on the teacher to help them scribe, spell, assemble and organise ideas. Others would be gaining confidence and growing in independence.

The rest of the class were doing activities that required less focused teacher support. One of the other non-focused groups was working at the computer. They were making a poster for the school's book week, and would print it out using the multi-font word processor. They were *practising the skills* of writing appropriated from the teacher's modelling and instruction. They could be seen spelling out words to each other, identifying letters on the keyboard, discussing layout, and so on. They were also *practising the social processes* of written language, exercised regularly in wider society but also contrived for pedagogical purposes by the teacher. Yet they had an authentic purpose for writing a poster and had been provided with a model of the form, and they knew it would have an authentic audience within the school.

INSIDE AND OUTSIDE THE SCHOOL

The theoretical framework of *Teach, Make Sense, Practise* allows the teacher to put into effect a variety of classroom organisational strategies which make effective use of her time and resources, not just in teaching writing but in other areas of the curriculum too.

Shared writing enables the teacher to model forms and purposes of writing that children may not yet have had the socio-cultural experience of practising. Writing news in the form we have just seen is not a common social practice, but it is the basis of writing social letters to family and friends or of writing a personal diary. Making a poster is an activity that may not arise commonly out of the day-to-day social processes of the home or school, though it is conceivable that some

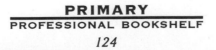

children may experience the need to do this if they or their families are involved in social activities at places of worship or local children's clubs.

Clearly, literacy practices and skills which never see life outside the classroom will only wither once they are exposed to the frosty conditions of literacy in wider social institutions and social processes. The literacy practices and skills that children learn at school and at home need to be 'hardened off' by real life and authentic interaction (as far as that is possible) with the literacy of the outside world. Literacy for its own sake is not enough. Teachers can and should help children and parents to create opportunities to practise literacy – not in the imitative sense of *practising* (the way one practises handwriting), but in the socio-cultural sense (as James Britton once put it, 'the way doctors practise medicine').

A major concern arising out of shared writing activities is the issue of making assessments and recording the progress of individual children. Some children choose to write regularly with a partner – indeed, their confidence and ability to compose any writing at all may depend on this hard-won condition. Many teachers go to great lengths to instil confidence in reluctant writers by encouraging them to compose a piece of writing with the teacher acting as the scribe of their ideas. Alternatively or additionally, organising shared writing in pairs of peers (particularly with self-selected friends) is another strategy that teachers regularly use to get children to produce more than they would be able to produce on their own.

WRITING IS A DIALOGUE

In many ways, all writing can be said to be an expression of fundamentally dialogic and social processes. One of the aims of the Shared Writing Project[12] (described on pages 134–139) was to shift the definition of a writer away from the traditional one of an individual working on his or her own towards one which saw the writer, even if he or she was working alone, as part of a wider literate community within which the individual writer is apprenticed. It also tried to shift the definition of writing away from the traditional view of it as a single-handed act of creation towards a more socio-cultural definition which took into account the way that genres of writing, as a socially constructed resource, provide a scaffold for apprentice writers to work within but have the potential to be objects of critical analysis and deconstruction.

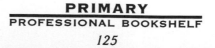

Let us explain. Obviously, we are not born as writers: we become writers. One of the ways that we become writers is through the acknowledgement and recognition of others that what we do counts as writing. The most powerful way that others do this is by responding to what we write, just as others responding to what we say tells us that what we are doing counts as talking. A response to writing can, of course, range from reading a memo and frowning silently to feeling excited about the arrival of a love letter, making an angry phone call in response to a demanding bill or changing the pattern of one's life after reading an Earth-shattering philosophical treatise.

Writing begins as a dialogue with oneself that has the potential, and often the intention, for dialogue with others. But if we want to be recognised as writers, we have to be seen in that position by our peers and perhaps even by a wider audience. For children, of course, others responding to the fledgling texts they produce is crucially important if they are to gain the confidence to say to themselves that it was worth the effort, not only for themselves as writers but for others as readers. They can only know that it was worthwhile if their teachers, parents and peers respond in some way – by praising, laughing, disagreeing, frowning, being moved, replying, displaying, publishing or whatever else is appropriate. It is not enough to tell young children that they can write and that they are writers: they will not believe you unless it is reflected in the social processes of their lives and those of people around them at home and at school.

The second way that we become writers is that we are apprenticed and instructed into the art or the craft. We don't teach ourselves to write. We are, by and large, taught how to do it – by teachers, parents and peers. We are taught how to hold paintbrushes, pencils and pens, and how to use keyboards. We are taught how to draw pictures, shape letters, move in a particular direction, write in lines, turn pages. We are taught how to remember the patterns and spellings of words we use, how to create effects by punctuation and other techniques, and how to recognise and use structures and styles. In other words, we initially appropriate the skills of others for ourselves by imitating them until we feel we have sufficient mastery to be confident, competent and independent users of them. But we do not invent these skills and technologies for ourselves. We do not need to: they are passed on to us by the keepers of our culture, who include our teachers and parents.

A third factor in our becoming writers is the ways that writing is required of us through the social, economic, legal and other demands it makes on the conditions of our full participation in society. The expectation that we will be required to engage in the social processes, structures and institutions of our society is enormous, and bears down on us from an early age. (One of the authors remembers that, as a six-year-old, the condition for joining the local library was being able to read a half-page of Enid Blyton's *Noddy* and write your full name unaided.) Happily, this is largely a thing of the past; but many schools still restrict their own libraries to the children who have worked their way far enough through the school reading scheme to be defined as 'free readers'. It is still very widespread practice for children to be given writing books only when they know the approved letters and sounds. Conditions such as these have a powerful effect on motivating us to project ourselves into the social processes of literacy. They can also serve to demotivate us and project us into a disastrous isolation from these social processes. David Barton[13] asserts that the very act of reading or writing takes on a symbolic function in the social context to which it relates: it can be an act of defiance or of solidarity, an act of conformity or a symbol of change. Our identities are expressed through literacy.

The writing that we produce as children and adults also needs to be seen in this socio-cultural context. We produce writing, not as instinctive acts of creation in a neutral isolation, but for a social purpose. (Even diaries, in my view, are a dialogue with oneself and therefore have a 'social other'.) We write to complain, to narrate, to enquire, to greet, to sympathise, to gossip, to request, to protest, to inform, and so on. We identify a purpose of communicating within the context of the social processes that have bearing upon us at any given time. Children who are helped to identify authentic purposes for writing have a very powerful cultural tool at their disposal. They know that such things as letters are a powerful medium within our social structure. A letter of complaint to a public body is registered; a

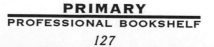

letter to a public company requesting information for a class project gets a response; a letter of protest to a newspaper or magazine may be published; a letter to a children's TV programme may be read out on the air.

Perhaps the most obvious way in which all the writing we do as children or adults is contextualised socio-culturally is by the way it is framed for the audience to whom it is being addressed. In identifying our audiences, we are required to make choices about the form our writing will take. We would not send posters to our friends to invite them to our birthday party when invitation cards or letters are the appropriate generic form for such a message. Nor would we apply for a job by sending a poetic narrative of our life history when a listed *curriculum vitae* is what is expected. In knowing our audience, we are guided and perhaps even governed by the social expectations of the generic form of writing: the genre. In one sense this is constraining, but genres also provide us with tools to manipulate the forms of writing available to us.

These forms of writing, though crucially influenced by the audience, are not created by us single-handedly. They are, like other aspects of writing, passed on to us. Children's exposure to a variety of literary forms of writing depends on the mediation of them – largely, it has to be said, in classrooms. Most children will meet poetry, narrative fiction, plays and non-fiction information texts (such as atlases and dictionaries) largely as a result of the experience of schooling, but there is a great variety of other forms of writing that children might have the opportunity to use both in and outside the classroom. Lists, letters, greetings cards, recipes, notes, signs, diaries, ledgers, financial transactions, bureaucratic forms and many more documents can be authenticated or meaningfully contrived to provide children with as many forms of writing as possible, in order to engage them with the social processes of their culture. Some teachers see this as a 'preparation' for the adult 'working' world. We prefer to see writing as a medium for engagement in the social processes of peer and public society that have begun to have a bearing on children's lives.

Writing should not be seen as a preparation for life, but as part of life. It is part of our job as teachers to identify where these purposes, audiences and forms cohere with the experiences of children, and to create opportunities for children to engage with them. The context of the school can be a forum for such opportunities. Writing in the context of the home arguably has much greater potential, and may also have the advantage of being authentic rather than contrived for the purposes of schooling.

THE BACKGROUND TO SHARED WRITING

Though there is a considerable history of practical schemes and research into parental involvement in reading[14] and in maths,[15] there is virtually no history at all, at least in this country, of research which looks at the development of writing in the context of the home. Intervention projects such as ALBSU's Developing Family Literacy initiative, launched in February 1995, went some way to redress this issue by offering a free activities pack to parents which accompanied a series of training videos on developing reading, writing and talk within the context of the family. Evaluation of that project and further research are currently under way. Apart from some other small-scale projects, writing has remained the 'great uncharted territory' of parental involvement. Why?

The first reason is that the controversies about methods and standards in reading dominate debates not only about literacy, but about education generally. Second, the attainment of reading is widely thought of as the defining achievement of learning at primary school; few teachers or parents put any other achievement higher than this. Third, the teaching of writing is an area of the curriculum that most teachers feel less confident about than the teaching of reading. Also, writing is an area where the influence of developmental and emergent literacy practices are less widespread, and consequently, teachers feel much less confident about subjecting their professional practices to the additional scrutiny that inevitably results from parental involvement schemes. Fourth, it is generally easier to assess reading and evaluate parental involvement reading schemes than it is to assess writing. Children's reading can be subjected to a variety of tests, however inadequate these may be, as a quantifiable measure of progress. Both teachers and parents can also make qualitative assessments of children's attitudes towards and enthusiasm for books. Writing is more complex in

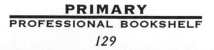

that, unless the focus is on the transcriptional aspects of the activity such as spelling and handwriting, assessment requires more aesthetic and value-laden judgements about the compositional aspects of content, style and structure.

Even though there is now considerable evidence that involving parents in the curriculum can produce a variety of benefits for all concerned, there are many teachers who are yet to be persuaded or feel that it is appropriate only in some areas, such as reading, maths or extracurricular activities. Writing seems to be one of these areas where many teachers feel that their professional judgements and practices are not easily transferable to parents. The view that parents may do more harm than good is still very prevalent, and was a marked feature in the early days of many parental involvement projects in reading and maths. This view persists even in schools where parental involvement is well established, though there is little evidence that what parents do with their children at home is in any way 'harmful', or even less beneficial than what teachers do with them at school. In many respects, especially where the quality and quantity of interaction is concerned, the opposite can be very powerfully argued.[16]

What, then, are the reasons for involving parents in writing activities that centre on the home? First, the home provides a context that children can easily make sense of. They are more familiar with the home surroundings and have greater access to its resources; there is a high adult-child ratio there, and the possibility that the child will have extended periods of 'quality time' in the company of a 'significant other'. In this context, therefore, the mediation of home-focused writing activities provides enormous opportunities to enhance literacy learning.

Second, this opportunity for enhanced literacy learning can help to prevent under-achievement. This must be a particular concern for educators in a society where literacy is unevenly distributed — especially in relation to social class — and where there is every likelihood that, with the advent of home-focused computer technology, this inequality will increase dramatically in the near future. One hardly needs to speculate that for the foreseeable future, the availability and use of CD-ROM will be heavily skewed towards those who can afford the technology and therefore the literacy. (We will return to this issue later.)

Third, it helps parents become more confident about improving their own basic skills – a factor which family literacy projects in this country and the United States have been keen to emphasise. Parents reporting on their involvement testify to the confidence it has given them in their own reading and writing, and to the interest it has aroused in continuing their learning.[17]

Finally, parental involvement schemes help parents learn ways of helping their own children by making conceptual connections not only between reading and writing, but between other areas of learning, such as maths, and other areas of their social experience, such as shopping, watching television, housekeeping, gardening or car maintenance.

There are, of course, some difficulties in trying to launch parental involvement schemes. At the least, many schools have been wary of entrusting parents with what they see as delicate professional practices. For example, when shared reading schemes were being established, many teachers and schools were unsure of the value of parents reading to children in ways that might conflict with the teaching methods and practices of the school. It is still common for schools to have parents' evenings 'to teach' parents how to read with their children and to offer them advice in booklets about how to sit, what books to choose, the length of time to be spent reading and what to do if children stumble over words. Teachers' expectations of parents' ability to engage in certain activities with their children, particularly in relation to literacy, are very varied.[18] Some teachers in schools that were initially approached for the piloting of the Shared Writing Project materials (discussed later in this chapter)[19] remarked on 'widespread illiteracy' among parents and stated that a high proportion of parents did not have English as their first language. It is difficult to know how much of this was an assumed perception and how much was based on informed knowledge. Nevertheless, there was a clear paradox in that these were teachers who had already established the IMPACT maths scheme in the school and had a long history of sending reading books home, in English, to the same parents that they assumed were either illiterate or having inadequate literacy in English to help their children with writing tasks. Explanations from the project team that this was 'not a writing in English project, but a writing project in any language' failed to reassure, and some teachers rejected the offer because they 'did not want to put parents in an embarrassing position'.

On the one hand, teachers should be seriously applauded for being sensitive to the possibility that the 'homework' activities that can be sent from the school have the potential for being socially divisive in the family, or that they might place parents in an 'embarrassing' position. On the other hand, teachers could be making some very far-reaching assumptions, both about literacy within families and about the dynamics of family life, which are not only inaccurate but are serving to deny the teachers and the families valuable learning opportunities. With sensitive support and encouragement, parents who are lacking in confidence about their own literacy may find the launch of such a scheme a rewarding opportunity. There are very few families who are so completely illiterate that there is no member at all who is willing to be engaged in some way in supporting their child's early writing or reading. As was found to be the common case with the IMPACT maths project, it is often a grandparent, older sibling or member of the extended family who becomes the helper for the activity. Some teachers report that, especially in the case of children who have English as a second language, it is much more likely that an older brother or sister will be the helper.

If such schemes are preceded by helpful support and encouragement for parents, providing even basic advice, then this could substantially increase the take-up rate. Many parents are unaware that the simple praise and appreciation of their child's drawings and scribbles and the plentiful provision of paper, pencils and crayons can have a dramatic effect on their child's orientation towards literacy.

Some schools have abandoned their parental involvement schemes because they felt that parents were not reflecting the practices of the school and were choosing inappropriate books, modelling undesirable and unhelpful decoding strategies, becoming too anxious, pressurising their children and making a variety of other mistakes. There is a widespread view that although parents are welcome to support what goes on in school, that support has to be clearly defined and contained – perhaps restricted to helping out at school fairs, accompanying classes on outings and so on. The feeling that, as far as the teaching of a curriculum area such as reading or writing is concerned, 'teachers know best' is still very widespread among both teachers and parents.

The authors have attended many meetings in schools over the years that have been characterised by some parents making apparently 'negative' comments about the introduction of a home-school project. Typical of such responses are the following:

> 'I don't have time to do all of this.'
> 'All they want to do is watch television.'
> 'I thought teaching them to read and write was your job, not mine!'

It would be very unwise for us as teachers to infer from such comments that the parents who made them do not care about the education of their children. People express their anxieties in a variety of often defensive ways, and what parents actually mean may be quite different from what they say. It may be, of course, that many parents have little confidence in their own literacy and are unsure how they can help their children learn to read and write when they have few uses for those practices themselves.

Compelling evidence from family literacy projects and research in the United States[20] points to the view that effort is maximised when teachers work closely with families to understand the literacy practices of the home and build the confidence of parents as well as that of the children. Denny Taylor's work is an inspiring testament to the determination of families living in poverty to make literacy accessible to their children; but as we know, literacy is not equitably distributed throughout society, and so the role of teachers and schools can make a difference. Schools in the UK, particularly in areas where high levels of socio-economic need are correlated with low levels of literacy attainment, have begun family literacy programmes which involve parents in separate and joint literacy activities with their children in school.[21] If the evidence from the US is anything to go by, family literacy initiatives may point the way to important new developments in the resourcing of schools to raise achievement in literacy for the future.

THE SHARED WRITING PROJECT

One of the very few projects which has looked specifically at writing in the context of the home has been the Shared Writing Project. Following on from the success of the IMPACT Project,[22] it used the same basic techniques of preparing activities for teachers to send home with children on a weekly or fortnightly basis. The activities are designed to be collaborative writing tasks, shared between a child and an adult helper or older sibling. For ease of discussion, all these will be referred to as 'parent', though in practice this is often not the case: the helper is frequently an older brother or sister, grandparent, relative or even babysitter. The activities are evaluated by parents and children in an accompanying diary.

The activities can be used as a starting-point for work in the classroom which is followed up in the home, or used for the first time in the home and followed up by work in the classroom as the teacher responds to issues that have arisen out of the children taking a particular activity home that week. Therefore, the model of the project (see Figure 5) shows an interaction between school-located, home-located, school-focused and home-focused activities.

In this respect, the project is attempting an important innovation. Though writing is deeply embedded in the everyday social practices of families and homes (from sending greetings cards, notes, reminders and letters to filling forms, paying bills, writing cheques and so on), the dominant definitions of literacy in society are still those that derive from school – that is, the ability to write narratives, reports and essays. So what counts as literacy at home is often at odds with what counts as literacy in school.[23] In helping teachers to reflect on the purposes, forms and audiences for writing, the project is attempting to help them embrace the home-based literacies which are reflected in the social practices of families, homes and communities, as well as the school-based literacies which reflect the pedagogic, social and even political and economic agendas of schools, LEAs and the National Curriculum.

The project itself was relatively small-scale, using eight pilot schools: four in inner-city locations where the majority of children were either bilingual, biliterate or exposed to languages other than English; two in county towns; and two in rural settings where the vast majority of children had English as their only language.

Figure 5

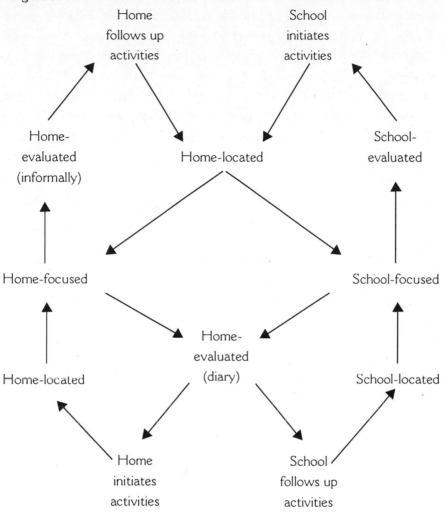

The project model shown in Figure 5 is constructed on the basis that activities
+ will be initiated primarily in the school;
+ will take place in the context of the home;
+ will be shared with a parent or adult helper;
+ will be evaluated at home by the child and the parent;
+ may be followed up or extended in the context of the school.

In writing the activity materials for the Shared Writing Project, we were aware of the need to provide and illustrate the widest possible variety of writing opportunities, forms and functions. We were concerned that the range of activities should embrace and reflect aesthetic as well as functional purposes. We anticipated some difficulty in providing as wide a variety of activities on 'imaginative writing' (such as narrative or poetry) as on 'functional writing' (such as lists, recipes or instructions), because it is more difficult to relate and locate an activity of imaginative writing in the context of the home. Writing narratives and poetry are associated much more with school-based practices than with home-based ones; in the home, functional writing such as greetings on birthday and festival cards, lists and letters tends to predominate.

The paradox for educators involved in such schemes is that by 'importing' activities which are predominantly associated with the school into the context of the home they are, in one sense, 'colonising' the home by transforming certain family-oriented, home-focused socialising practices into school-oriented, pedagogically focused ones. For example, a parent writing a shopping list may or may not be aware of the potential for using this functional social practice to develop literacy, another functional social practice, in their children. Whether or not they are aware of it, the nature and form of that practice (within the family) is distinct from the same practice if it were suggested as a pedagogical activity, imported into the home from the school. The school's expectations of parents and children and the parents' expectations of themselves in such a context become quite complex. Is the parent expected to take on the role of a teacher? Is the child expected to take on the role of a teacher? Is the activity open to the kind of negotiation that may be tolerated in the home but not in the school, such as 'Can I do it after watching *Neighbours*?' or 'Can I write in my orange felt-tip pen?'

In one school in Haringey, North London that served as a pilot for the Shared Writing Project, two Year Four teachers had decided to prioritise homework as part of a policy to promote home-school liaison. There was already regular contact between the teachers and parents in the school, partly through the fortnightly IMPACT Maths activities going home and partly through the efforts teachers made to inform parents of curricula and social events in the school.

IMPACT Maths activities were already established as an 'essential part of the classroom routine'. When introducing the Shared Writing activities the teachers insisted on participation, ensuring that the children were well briefed about the activities before they went home. They had previously made it clear to parents that their children would be expected to do the activities during play and lunch times if they were unable to find a helper at home. As a result, they had 'virtually a 100% response rate'; and as the incidence of children that were unable to find a helper to share the activities with varied from week to week, they felt that they were justified in this particular prescription. Clearly, there are ethical questions about how compulsory one can make homework, especially when it relies on the recruitment of either an adult or an older sibling; but one teacher remarked that 'if you're going to take something like this seriously, there is no point in having it any other way'.

The first Shared Writing activity that the teachers sent home was to find the longest word on the breakfast cereal packet and use it to generate as many words as possible. This is a simple, well-known word game that many teachers and children are familiar with. The activity met with unanimous enthusiasm from children and parents. Another activity sent home involved sequencing pictures. The teachers had photocopied a wordless six-paneled picture story they had found in some materials prepared for Turkish bilingual children. As usual, they had prepared the children by discussing in some detail what the task involved – in this case, making up a story to match the pictures and writing it, with help, in the language of their choice. The pictures could be sequenced in a variety of ways to allow for a number of stories to be told, and the teachers had demonstrated one such example before the children went home.

The importance of demonstrating the activity before children go home is a feature of the IMPACT process that teachers emphasise repeatedly. Many teachers report that not only does this reduce the possibility of misunderstanding, it often removes altogether the need for the parent to read the activity sheet and interpret the instructions.

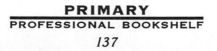

Instead, the child becomes the instructor and takes on the powerful role of leading the activity by explaining the purpose and the process. This structure, which is a feature of the way teachers themselves have interpreted IMPACT, has placed the child in the role of the tutor.

When the children returned with the picture-sequencing and story-writing activity the following week, the teachers discovered that stories had been written in eleven languages other than English, some of which they had been unaware of as the home language of particular children. They were especially pleased about the discovery of writing abilities in one child who had helped his father write the story in Arabic, but had previously not written in English and had been assumed to be a non-writer. For one teacher, this was a catalyst for action, not just to find out more about the children's linguistic and cultural background to develop the school's records but also for work with the children on language awareness. She reported that

> Each activity gives at least a whole lesson and fills 'Show and Tell' in assembly. Each one could be a project.

A colleague added:

> I've got some children for whom IMPACT, Shared Writing and the Diary is by far the best work they do. One child I can think of gets so much more work done at home than at school. And parents are really pleased with it, you get that back from them all the time.

Indeed, one of the diary entries for this activity was from a Greek-speaking parent who had helped her son write the story in Greek:

> This is a very good experience for my son. He likes it alot and so did I.

Reporting back, some teachers found that the most successful activities were those that generated lists rather than narratives, commenting that such activities were easier to follow up, review and evaluate as a whole group in the class. Some teachers chose activities because they complemented some aspect of the current curriculum topic – for example, a group of parallel year classes doing a half-term topic on colour reported the success of an activity entitled 'Invisible Colour'. The task involved describing the physical features, but not the colours, of fruits and vegetables found at home.

At other times, the same teachers reported choosing activities that could be adapted to topical events, issues and festivals. For example, some activities create opportunities for writing various kinds of recipes and menus, and some teachers reported enthusiasm and a high response rate when menu activities were sent home at Christmas and Eid. For others, the opportunity to reinforce school-based language teaching was the focus of some of the activities chosen. In one case, a teacher reported looking through the activity pack to find one that directly supported the teaching point he had addressed in his language activities in the class that week, which had dealt with adjectives. He reported a very high rate of enthusiasm for the activity asking 'How many words can you think of that mean the same as *big*?' He also commented on how this activity was the occasion for a considerable amount of discussion about bilingualism. Some children from bilingual households had returned with words in Greek and Turkish, while one boy 'really surprised and impressed everyone' by offering the French *grand* in the follow-up session in class.

INVOLVING PARENTS IN SHARED WRITING: GETTING STARTED

Launching a parental involvement project can be an exciting venture that will mobilise, motivate and unite a school staff around a common goal. As with any project, success depends on a clear purpose, adequate planning, preparation and a commitment to succeeding. This section offers some ideas and advice about getting started.

The setting up of parental involvement projects presents a number of conceptual questions which need to be addressed from the outset. It is not essential to resolve them all before launching a project; but if they cannot be resolved, teachers and parents need to be aware of the shortcomings of the model. This might prevent confusion, misunderstanding and

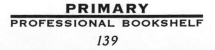

frustration later on. Discussion and attempts at clarification of the following need to be made explicit.

First, *how will the project be launched?* How will it be explained to parents? Parental involvement schemes need to get off to a good start, and so a launch meeting where parents are made to feel relaxed and welcome, possibly with food and drink, is a good idea. Launching a project to promote parental involvement in writing may need extra preparation because of the problematic nature of explaining to parents the teaching approaches taken by the school — for example, if a 'developmental' approach is favoured, will the school need to explain the value of invented spellings in early writing or the value of a shared piece of writing which is composed by the child but scripted by an adult? Will the project be supported by a booklet or some form of additional information for parents unable to attend a launch meeting or for reference later? Will the booklet be published in languages other than English?

Second, *what is the context for the activities? Is it the home, the school or both?* The pedagogic and social practices of the home are very different from those of the school, and both the child's and the adult's responses will be largely determined by the context. For example, a teacher will employ a specific set of strategies for teaching a child to read at school; but when she returns home as a parent, she may well decide that these are not appropriate strategies for her own child in the context of the home.

Third, *is the nature of the activity related (or oriented) to the context?* For example, does the activity draw on behaviour or resources that can only be found at home, such as playing a word game derived from a television quiz show or using words selected from a breakfast cereal packet? Or is it an activity that reflects the pedagogic practices of school, such as a phonic awareness activity like making a list of words that begin with *sh*?

Fourth, *who will be asked to do the activities?* Will it be the whole school, or just some classes? Will some classes 'blaze the trail' by pioneering certain activities, and others follow on later? Nurseries and infant classes have a much higher rate of take-up and participation than most junior classes, even within the same school. Will all the children do the activities, or only those identified as having special remedial needs? Clearly, identifying children and parents on the basis of special need can become problematic – though given sensitive consultation with parents and other involved agencies such as the Schools Psychological Service, a limited parental involvement scheme on this basis may be justified.

Fifth, *how long will it last and how frequent will it be?* Parental involvement schemes are notoriously demanding of time, energy and commitment on the part of teachers as well as parents. Should the scheme run for a limited period at times of the year when staff can give it a high priority, or should it run indefinitely but perhaps require regular inputs and refreshers? Should the activities be taken home nightly, weekly, fortnightly?

Sixth, *what personnel and material resources will be needed?* Will it need a named co-ordinator to be responsible? How much time can teachers spare to meet concerned parents or respond to diaries? How much photocopying or printing will be needed?

Seventh, *who will evaluate the activities? The teacher, the parent, the child or a combination of these?* Many schemes, including the Shared Writing Project, involve an evaluation diary which has space for the child and the parent to evaluate the activity and for the teacher to respond.

Eighth, *are the activities either culturally specific or culturally exclusive?* Do they rely on asking children to comment on or discuss with parents matters that may be inappropriate for certain cultural or religious groups? For example, some activities in the Shared Writing Project ask children to discuss controversial issues such as the banning of smoking in public places and to construct arguments for and against. Some activities ask parents and children to make birthday calendars. Neither of these is unproblematic, in that in some contexts they may conceivably be both culturally inappropriate and socially divisive.

Some activities ask children to write letters. Evidence from the project and from elsewhere[24] shows that for some families, notably those deriving from the Indian subcontinent, a letter is much less likely to be from one person to another than to be from one family to another. It will probably be scribed by one person for the whole family, include the views, news and gossip of the whole family and, when

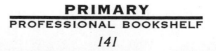

received, be read aloud by one person to the whole of the receiving family. Discovering interesting and culturally diverse literacy practices can not only inform teachers but add an unexpected dimension to parental involvement projects.

Ninth, *is the choice of activities related to the gender of the children?* Girls are now scoring higher than boys in nearly all tests in primary and secondary schooling. Boys and girls tend to write about different things. Like much else, the practices of literacy are gendered. What are the implications of this for writing activities done at home?

Additionally, one should ask *whether the activities are socially biased.* As we have already noted, literacy is unevenly distributed within society. Do the activities rely on access to such things as dictionaries, thesauruses, encyclopaedias, computers or other resources that may be unevenly distributed among the families of children in a socially or ethnically mixed school? This is a particular dilemma for literacy schemes, because part of the value of such a scheme is its ability to draw on the resources that exist outside the school and to maximise the opportunities for children to experience the widest possible variety of print literacy and other media literacies. But there is a paradox in this: the more the school turns to the home to maximise these opportunities, the more the unequal distribution of literacy experiences may be entrenched.

WORKSHOP EVENTS

We have observed or organised a variety of gatherings and events in schools over recent years. Some of the most successful have been the kind of literacy workshop described in Chapter 2, where part of the school (usually the hall) has been converted into various rooms of a home. The opportunities for reading and writing are made explicit or realistically contrived, and parents and children are guided to engage in as many activities as possible. For example, in 'the lounge' there were postcards, greetings cards and stationery to write on and send to relatives and friends. The children were also encouraged to add their addresses to an address book that was provided. A diary and wall calendar were on hand for children to find and write in family birthdays. A Polaroid camera was available for children to take a family portrait, make a card frame, write an accompanying caption and send it to a relative. A member of staff, positioned in the school office, continually rang an extension phone situated in 'the lounge'; children were encouraged to answer it and, with the help of their parents, to take a (contrived) message and deliver it to another member of staff. Similarly, there was a range of possible writing activities in the other rooms.

Other events have included ideas such as assembling a writing 'tool kit' comprising various pencils, pens, felt-tips, a note-pad, a note-book, scrap paper, envelopes, a pencil sharpener, an eraser and a list of addresses that children could write to for free information. Parents were asked to contribute a small sum towards the cost of the contents and to take the 'tool-kit' home in a decorated shoe box or plastic tool holder (available inexpensively from hardware stores). Many schools have staged book-making evenings, where stories have been told to provide the stimulus for parents and children to make simple concertina, zig-zag or stapled books of children's retellings scribed by their parents.

An idea used by another school was to demonstrate to parents the use of 'response partners' in children's writing. This strategy is used widely in classrooms, and is derived and adapted from Donald Graves'[25] pioneering work on writing conferences. In a simplified form, it involves making some supportive comments and asking some brief but sympathetic questions about a child's writing. For example, at one meeting parents were shown a short school-made video of one of the teachers discussing writing with a group of children. Comments and questions followed a pattern:

◆ a positive comment from the adult to a child saying why they had enjoyed it,

'This letter sounds just like you, it's really good!'

◆ a question asking the child to comment positively on the writing,

'What do you like about it? Tell me.'

✦ an additional positive comment from the adult, responding if possible to what the child has said – for example,

> 'I like that too, the way you have tried to put in a joke to make it sound friendly.'

✦ a question asking the child to be positively critical,

> 'If you could think of one way to improve your letter, what would it be?'

The strategy of 'response partners' is used much more extensively and in more sophisticated ways than this by many teachers in this country and in the United States,[26] particularly with older children. Some schools have found that while parents are willing to share and scribe their young children's writing, they are less willing to continue to do so as children mature and acquire the necessary physical dexterity and skills for themselves. Introducing parents to this strategy may serve as a useful starting-point for encouraging them to become involved collaboratively with their older children's writing in ways that might not occur to them normally.

CONCLUSIONS

At this point, it is necessary to raise two crucial points about the nature of literacy in relation to our discussion. The first is that because literacy is a social practice, it is bound to reflect social processes and social inequalities. We need to recognise that literacy for its own sake is not a self-evident 'good' or an automatic benefit to all people in society: it can be used as an instrument of oppression as well as liberation.[27] Indeed, if it serves to exacerbate social divisions, then we need to question what kinds of literacy are serving the social needs of particular groups. Secondly, because of the ideological nature of social processes, 'the literacy of the school' – with its emphasis on literacy rather than orality, on book-based knowledge, on Standard English and on literature – is much more likely to reflect and blend with the literacy of the middle-class home, the middle-class community and even the middle-class workplace.[28]

Homes are not only places where the fruitful mediation of signs occurs: they also have potential for a great variety of 'sign making' processes. Children are constantly making signs through their play — that is to say, they are making metaphors, making an object stand for something beyond itself. They will make Lego models of spaceships, turn pieces of wood into racing cars, turn their fingers into puppets, turn a bundled cardigan into a crying doll, turn a cardboard box into a house or cave; and they will scribble, draw, cut, stick and paint pictures of themselves and others. In the home, children may have a wider variety of sign-making opportunities open to them; they may have more time, more resources and more support. The evidence for this spans all social classes.

Schools, however, particularly beyond the nursery and reception years, are primarily concerned with sign-making in one mode of representation: print literacy. Granted, children will paint, draw, dance, make music and so on; but all the concern, time and resources put together for the promotion of these 'sign-making' activities will not equal that devoted to the development of print literacy through reading and writing. Learning to write is only one of the ways that we make signs and metaphors for meaning in our culture. Some would argue that it is the most important way, but that is for the users to decide; artists, musicians and dancers might well disagree. The metaphors for meaning in many homes may be dominated not by print or even by the 'media literacies' of TV, video, computers or multimedia, but by car mechanics, cooking, sport or gardening. One might easily expect a keen gardener, proud of the creative investment made in the design and nurturing of a beautiful garden, to argue powerfully that the meaning-making potential residing in the garden is, for her, much greater than that which resides in any printed text.

As teachers, we must be aware of the vast range of other sign-making, metaphoric practices available to human culture, and be aware that through over-emphasis on written literacy we may be reducing the opportunities for creativity and cross-fertilisation of symbolic forms. Children growing up and learning to compose music and dance are more open to this potential than those who are literate in

print only. Belatedly, in this country, we have discovered that bilingual children need to use their first language to learn their second, and then go on to use their second to reflect on their first. Their linguistic competence is only diminished by emphasising one language to the detriment of the other.

Literacy can maintain, challenge and change social processes and institutions. New literacies emerge and old ones die out. Children growing up in our time already know of the enormous potential for meaning-making in television, video and multimedia – not instead of print, but in addition to it. Their confidence with these new literacies threatens many of us. An overemphasis by teachers and parents on print literacy, or a lack of understanding of the potential other literacies have to offer, can result in children coming to view print literacy (in the words of Gunter Kress) as a 'semantically vacuous technology' which disastrously restricts and reduces the meaning-making opportunities for children.[29]

If our efforts in these parental involvement and curriculum intervention projects serve to shift parents' interaction with their children too far towards traditional definitions of literacy and narrow purposes of writing which do not embrace the real literacy practices and contexts of family life, then we will be doing a disservice to children, to parents and perhaps even to family life itself. We need to understand when and where we are needed and wanted as teachers, and when and where we are not. We need to be ready to change our practices where necessary to take account of practices in homes, families and communities. These can inform and enrich the way we teach; and even given the political constraints of the National Curriculum, this is both a worthy challenge and an achievable goal.

REFERENCES

1 Michael Stubbs (1980 & 1983) has written a number of useful linguistics books for teachers. These are two which readers will find interesting.
2 Myra Barrs wrote a fascinating study of a small boy's drawings while on holiday (in Meek & Mills, 1988).

3 For an excellent introduction to writing see Temple *et al* (1982 & 1988).

4 Ferreiro and Teberovsky's (1982) study of pre-schoolers has had an enormous influence on perceptions of young children's access to literacy before school.

5 See the chapter on 'The Pre-History of Written Language' in Vygotsky (1978).

6 See Chapter 9 of Kress (1994).

7 For greater depth on this issue, see Clay (1975) and Temple *et al* (1982 & 1988). For a good summary, see Browne (1993).

8 Gelb (1963) quoted in Barton (1994).

9 Such as Tizard and Hughes (1984) and Minns (1990).

10 Ann Browne's book on writing (1993) gives a very useful summary of these headings, with some interesting examples.

11 See Chapter 3 of Smith (1982).

12 See the papers delivered at the AERA Annual Meeting in San Francisco (1995) by Merttens and Newland, available from the IMPACT Office, University of North London.

13 Barton (1994) p 48.

14 See the various research reports on home-school reading projects such as Tizard *et al* (1982), Griffiths and Hamilton (1984), Topping and Wolfendale (1985) and Hannon and Jackson (1987).

15 See Merttens and Vass (1990 & 1993).

16 See especially Chapter 3 in Hannon (1995).

17 See the Family Literacy video and materials from ALBSU (1995).

18 See Chapter 2 of Hannon (1995).

19 See Merttens, Newland and Webb (in print – not yet published).

20 Denny Taylor gives a number of accounts of working with families in poverty in the US. One of the most vivid is co-authored with Catherine Dorsey-Gaines (1988).

21 See the Family Literacy video and materials from ALBSU (1995).

22 See Merttens and Vass (1990 & 1993).

23 David Barton's book (1994) provides some interesting discussion of the contexts and discourses of literacy.

24 See the fascinating chapter on the literacies of Punjabi speakers in Southall by Saxena in Hamilton *et al* (1994).

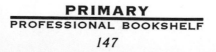

25 Donald Graves' book (1983) made a huge impact on the teaching of writing in the US and the UK in the mid-1980s.

26 See Graves (1983) and Calkins (1994) for more about this useful technique.

27 See Paolo Frière (1972) for more about the politics of literacy and its role in liberation politics.

28 Hannon (1995) p 14.

29 Kress (1994) p 220.

PARENTAL INVOLVEMENT IN THE WIDER CURRICULUM

The longest journey begins with one step.
Chinese proverb

We have discussed the involvement and participation of parents in their children's learning to talk, to read, to write, and to do mathematics. Many would suggest that the whole thing should stop there. Teachers have enough to do, it is argued, in thinking about and planning for the children without thinking about the parents as well. However, there can be positive advantages for teachers, with respect to both the quantity and the quality of their work, in inviting parental collaboration in the other areas of the curriculum.

One of the major factors in this debate concerns the school's general approach to education. There are two conflicting ideals of education which schools can choose to project to the children and the parents. They can convey a view of education as a form of training. Alternatively, they can convey a sense of education as a 'leading out', or 'drawing out' as the etymology of the word itself suggests to us (from 'ducare', the Latin verb meaning 'to lead', and 'e', the Latin prefix meaning 'out of'). Both of these ideas are often present, covertly if not overtly, in the current debates about education – in the political arena as well as among the general public. However, the messages that we communicate to parents have, we would argue, a more than transient effect on the children's educational expectations, as well as on the general political and educational climate.

EDUCATION AS TRAINING

There has been a tendency in recent years to focus on the 'vocational' aspects of education, seeing education in general and schools in particular increasingly as sites where we provide children with skills which will

prepare them to do specific jobs. The difficulty with this view of schooling, pleasingly efficient though it often sounds, is that not only is it hard to tell which children are going to do which jobs, but also we are no longer sure what jobs will be available when the children hit the job market, and so we cannot be sure what skills they will require.

There are theoretical difficulties with this model of education as well. The idea that skills acquired in one context can be utilised in another is more contested than it used to be,[1] and the whole notion of decontextualised skills which are transferable from one situation to another has been found, in empirical research, to be an unsatisfactory metaphor and one which does not help us to interpret the data.[2] However, notwithstanding these hiccups, this view of education has gained in popularity, particularly with reference to secondary and post-secondary education.

Several implications follow from the belief that to educate someone is to train them in specific skills or competencies. The emphasis on 'real-life' activities – that is, tasks and problems which children will encounter in the course of 'everyday life' – has its origin in the view that education is primarily about competencies. Children need to become competent functioning adults in our society, goes the argument, and it is the job of schools and teachers to help them achieve this. The notion of 'authentic' activities[3] or tasks which are genuinely part and parcel of school life – such as planning a school trip or designing a new playground area – also has its provenance in this pragmatic approach to education.

EDUCATION AS A 'LEADING OUT'

This view of education is predicated on a sense that a person's education is never complete, and also that education is fundamentally a *social process*. The beliefs implicit in this construction of what it is to educate someone are complex and not easily summarised. So in attempting to define this particular view of education, we can do a lot worse than to look at the margins, at those on the 'edges' of education, and at how the boundaries are constructed.

In 1995, at a large gathering of educational researchers from many different countries, all of whom were concerned with parental participation in the schooling processes, a researcher from the USA education department gave a very interesting presentation.[4] He had been concerned with looking at the fate of those children who had been educated by their parents at home. In England and Wales, these children and their parents mostly fall under the umbrella of an organisation called 'Education Otherwise' – so called because the 1944 Education Act specified that parents had a duty to ensure that their children attended school, or to provide for their 'education otherwise'. The researcher had considered the cognitive attainment of children educated at home in both Canada and the USA, and compared their attainment with that of comparable groups of children educated in the conventional manner through the state schools.

The findings made interesting reading. In the USA, many parents will educate their children at home for religious reasons. This is because the state schools are, by law, wholly non-religious. There is no religious dimension to the school curriculum in the public (i.e. state) schools. This has the effect of encouraging many devoutly Christian families (both rich and poor) to keep their children out of a secular educational system and educate them at home in the religious community of which they are a part. Thus the home-educated children come from a much wider cross-section of the socio-economic community than would be common in the UK. The study had found that the working-class and black children – traditionally those sections of the population which are expected to succeed least well within the schooling system – were doing much better if they were educated at home. The same applied to all the cross-sections of the community. It was true for the middle-class and more well-to-do white children, but the difference was more noticeable for the economically 'disadvantaged' children. The presenter commented wryly that if his advice as a statistician were asked by parents, he would have to say that if you are not very well-to-do, you will do better to educate your children at home than to send them to school!

This raises precisely the questions of what a 'good' education consists in. The study mentioned had looked only at academic measures – how the children had performed in maths, English, science, and so on. It had not considered the social, emotional or spiritual needs or

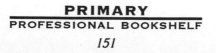

achievements of children. Many listeners expressed their disapproval of a judgement apparently made on the basis of an assumption that only one sort of attainment 'counted' in education. They felt that education was a much broader process, in which learning how to get on with your peers, how to live and work with people from a variety of different backgrounds and with different beliefs, and how to collaborate in solving a problem or achieving a result, were all crucially important. Cognitive or academic attainment, although obviously central, could not be held to be the only (or even the most important) criterion by which we should judge the quality of a child's education.

The idea that education is a 'leading out' is certainly not new. Philosophers and educationalists from Rousseau through the Enlightenment to Dewey and the post-Piagetian liberal psychologists have all, in different ways, argued for such a view. However, perhaps not until now have these ways of describing education been under threat, both theoretically and rhetorically. Sociologists have come to focus on schooling as social reproduction – the view that schools and the schooling process, through a series of complex and diverse mechanisms, serve to reproduce and maintain social inequalities.[5] By contrast, anthropologists stress the notion that schooling transmits culture – i.e. that all we learn in school is how to be good pupils, and that learning may best be viewed as an 'apprenticeship' where skills cannot be thought of as 'transferable' but must be acquired in the context of their use.[6]

In this situation it seems to us, as it does to many teachers, that it is important – not only for the profession but also for the children themselves – that we try to envisage schools as places where education in its broadest and most liberal sense can and does (sometimes!) take place. Teachers can provide much that homes – and even local communities – cannot. This is not because teachers are better or nicer or more moral or more clever than parents. It is precisely due to the context – physical, social and rhetorical – of the school as such. Teachers introduce children to aspects of life, to topics, to subjects and to practices which they simply would not meet in their daily communal lives. A teacher reads, teaches and writes poetry with children. She introduces them to art in many forms: clay, sculpture, modelling and screen-printing as well as painting. She does maths puzzles and games, and investigates the ways in which numbers work or patterns emerge. At school the children encounter not only other lifestyles and belief systems, exemplified through the other children, but also other possible *ways of being*.[7] They realise that they could be poets or scientists, artists or historians, even if there are none of these in the community in which their home is embedded.

The school, in this configuration of education, thus becomes a site in which potentialities may be explored and teachers may become sources of inspiration – not necessarily all the time (which is impossible!), but in certain ways and with reference to particular lessons. When the teacher reads some poems, discusses them with the children and then encourages them to produce their own poetry, she is demonstrating what it means to be a poet. When she does a piece of maths – shows them, for example, Pythagoras' theorem or Gauss' means of summing a series – she is demonstrating what it means to be a mathematician. And to do these things, the teacher does not need to be either a gifted poet or a brilliant mathematician. All she needs to be is a good teacher!

PARENTS AS PARTNERS

This view of education has important implications for parental involvement and for the ways in which teachers and parents can work together, not just in helping children to achieve the basic skills – reading, writing and mathematical – but also in terms of the wider curriculum, of their education in general. These implications can be categorised under three general points.

1. Education is an ongoing process. Not only are teachers educating children, they are also educating themselves. All teachers have experienced the feeling of pleasure gained from having worked out how to do something (such as marbling), or having increased their understanding through preparing a new topic (for example, on a local historical or ecological site). Parents, too, find that as their children are educated, their own education is advanced and expanded. This is a very useful facet of the situation, since children can be encouraged (through a variety of specific means) to share with their parents aspects of a topic in history, geography, science or technology.

2. Teachers do *not* know it all! Sometimes a parent may possess an expertise or an understanding of a particular area which can be very helpful in planning and delivering a particular topic. Parents can come into class to work with small groups of children, or to present some information or relate their experience to the whole class. The children are often much more stimulated to listen and put questions to the visitor than they would have been had the same information been provided by the teacher. Suggestions for ways of handling parental input, as well as areas in which their contribution is likely to be located, are given later in this chapter.

3. Study and research skills are often skills which children can acquire much more effectively when working at home, with their parents, than in the classroom. Learning how to use an index, how to look things up in a dictionary, and how best to organise notes can all be demonstrated by the teacher in class, but are best practised when the child is finding things out or reading something at home. The necessary reference books can be borrowed from the library or school and used at home. In this way, both the parents and the children can often discover things together.

RETURNING TO A MODEL OF CLASSROOM PRACTICE

Later in this chapter, we shall suggest ways in which all these ideas can be translated into classroom practices without requiring a great deal of time or energy to be invested by the teacher. However, at this point it is necessary to return to the model of classroom education which was outlined in the first chapter. For ease of reference, we repeat the outline on the opposite page.

WHERE DO PARENTS FIT IN?

Where do parents fit into this model of classroom education? Traditionally, as we mentioned in the first chapter, homework belonged in the 'practise' category. Once the children had been taught something in class, they took it home and practised it. Thus children would take home a page of sums or a page of 'copying out' — the kind of repetitive work which could just as easily have been done

---

TEACH

✦ Teachers actively instruct, narrate, model and explain.

MAKE SENSE

✦ Children make this knowledge their own, and make sense of what they have been taught through a variety of means, including stories, practical activities, problem-solving tasks, games, puzzles and investigative, exploratory and creative work.

PRACTISE

✦ Skills often require practice and reinforcement. This can be achieved through activities on an individual basis, in pairs and in small groups.

---

in class. Furthermore, in situations where the child had not understood the lesson, and had not grasped how the sums were to be done or what was to be copied, the parent was placed in the unenviable position of having to 'be the teacher'. This is inequitable in that some children have parents who are able, for whatever reason, both to do the sums and also to show their child how to do them. Other parents may well not be in this position. They may have failed at maths themselves, or not be sure *how* they do what they do. We are often able to do something without knowing how we do it or why the method works. For example, we can drive without knowing how the internal combustion engine works; or type on to a word-processor without having a clue how a computer functions. A child can speak grammatically without being able to articulate a single grammatical rule. So a parent who can do a page of sums may be in no position to explain to a child just how to do it.

Many classrooms, in the past, gave the 'Make sense' part of the model rather short shrift. There were few, if any, 'making sense' activities in the classroom in which I was educated. The teacher taught, we copied and then we practised. If you had not managed to make sense of what was taught, then tough! However, with twenty years of educational pressure from child psychologists and liberal educationalists, there are few classrooms nowadays where the teacher is not concerned whether children understand what they are doing. The OFSTED inspection schedule reinforces the importance of this aspect of classroom practice with its insistence on the quality of teaching *and learning*. However, many parents, educated as I was in classroom contexts notably lacking in this type of activity, are hard-pressed to understand what is going on in their children's classrooms.

Parents gravitate to the familiar, and feel bewildered and sometimes threatened by what is 'new', in education as elsewhere. However, it is also the case that 'making sense' of what they have learned, with the concomitant requirement of talking about it, is precisely what children do best at home. Thus if a child goes home and explains something to a parent, they are likely (in a very real sense) to make that knowledge their own. Homes, as we learned in the second chapter, provide a rich source of linguistic and intellectual stimulation; and the quality of the talk, and of the discursive encounters in general, is likely to be higher than in the school.[8] A child explaining a topic to a parent is a one-to-one meeting, in a way which is rare in the classroom context. The parent is also interested in the child's view, and, most likely, less concerned with her own agenda in the conversation than the teacher is. The conversation is child-led, and the interaction proceeds at the child's pace – again a sadly rare occurrence at school. In all, the conversation is more likely to be 'supportive' in style (see Gordon Wells' categories in Chapter 1) than 'didactic', which is going to enhance the child's learning and understanding – as well as, perhaps, that of the parents.

There has been considerable research into what is called 'peer tutoring',[9] where one child acts as a tutor to another in the course of a particular activity or task. It has been shown that, perhaps contrary to our expectations, it is the child doing the tutoring who is likely to gain the most. Explaining something to someone else is, as many teachers already know, the best way to come to understand it for yourself. Through their articulation of the reasons why no more sugar will dissolve in the beaker of water, or how it is that we have night and daytime, the children construct an explanation and make sense of it within the context of what they already know and the vocabulary and theories with which they are familiar.

The 'Practise' part of the model is also relevant to home-school collaboration. As was stated above, the traditional homework pattern is to give the children further examples of something they have been doing in class for them to continue at home. This is a pattern with which parents are very familiar. However, for all the reasons given, this can further disadvantage those children whose parents themselves failed at school and are not in a position to offer them assistance when it is needed. Also, these types of task in no way draw upon or utilise the context of the home. The child could be doing the page of sums in the classroom or on the moon, for all the difference it makes.

However, there are advantages to practising skills in the home, and to engaging parents' support at various stages in this process. It is useful, and arguably essential, to practise some skills in as wide a variety of different contexts as possible. The home provides an appropriate source of out-of-school situations. Also, with certain skills, especially those which rely heavily upon repetition or memory, children can be much more ably and effectively helped by parents or grandparents, or even older siblings, than they can by teachers in school. Learning the days of the week or the months of the year, learning how to write their own address and even learning how to tell the time may all fall into this category.

PRACTICAL SUGGESTIONS

Schools can implement a variety of practices which will help to convert the approach outlined above into real-life scenarios. We have categorised these under different subject headings.

SCIENCE

In 1989, the SHIPS (School-Home Investigations in Primary Science) project was set up by Joan Solomon at Oxford University.[10] Conceived

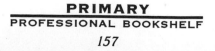

along the same lines as the IMPACT project in maths, SHIPS was concerned with working with teachers to involve parents in children's learning of science. The overt aim of SHIPS was to 'increase public understanding of science' at the same time as improving children's attainment in science work. Joan Solomon remarks that 'in purely physical terms it is clear that the activities take on the character and culture of the home'. The children doing a science activity in the context of their own kitchen, weighing bread as it dries out, testing different materials to see how 'stretchy' they are or growing a crystal, are far more likely to have enough time to reflect upon the processes involved and generate an explanation for them than if they were doing the same activity at school. The quality of this reflection, and of the dialogue with the parent about *why* what is happening occurs, is of a different order from that which is possible in the school setting. Not only are the children operating one-to-one, but they are able to mull over several possible explanations and try out possible theories without the fear of· looking foolish and of being 'wrong'.

The SHIPS project has now produced several books which provide a wide range of suitable science activities for children to take home and share with a parent, grandparent or sibling. These activities, published by the Association for Science Education, are widely available through bookshops and teachers' centres. Since the main benefits from shared science activities, as with shared maths and shared writing, are derived from the fact that the children can talk to a parent or other adult, the science task chosen by the teacher should require that the children explore a new idea rather than revise what is 'already known'. The project name does not contain the word 'investigation' for no reason. The children and their parents are being encouraged to think scientifically, in terms of exploring not just 'what happens' but 'why it happens'. Does their explanation fit the facts? Does it enable them to predict what would happen in another, similar circumstance? Both science as process and theory as a social construction are highlighted in this investigative and dialogic approach to science in the home.

There are clearly differences between the science and the maths or writing projects in terms of the perceptions of the parents and the resources needed to do the tasks. Although every effort is made by

those who created the activities to utilise only those things which would be found in most homes or would be easily available to the majority of parents, nonetheless it is inevitable, given the nature of the subject-matter, that some parents are going to find the demands made in terms of resources (spatial as well as material) are not ones which can be met within their current living conditions. In the IMPACT maths and Shared Writing projects described in Chapters 3 and 4, there are many activities which require nothing more than a pencil and the back of the piece of paper upon which the activity is outlined. In the science activities, this constraint is simply not possible, and the numbers of parents involved in particular areas may be affected as a consequence. However, schools keen to use these activities, and to involve parents in science in the same way that they do in maths and writing, have certainly found that, with encouragement and some careful selection of activities, the SHIPS approach can work very effectively with the majority of parents.

Many schools send home a couple of science activities a term, selecting these with their science topics in mind and replacing the IMPACT or Shared Writing activity with the science for that week. It is interesting that parents can be converted to these activities. At first, many parents think that the sorts of task suggested in the SHIPS books are 'not really science'. Science is all test-tubes and 'facts', for many parents whose memories of science consist of precisely those two things. The idea that learning science may involve teaching children how to come up with scientific explanations and models, and then testing these against their experiences, is still new in primary education. Furthermore, some parents are more inclined to think that science should happen exclusively in the classroom. They are persuaded that their help is necessary with the basics like reading, writing and arithmetic – but when it comes to science, that is surely the teacher's job.

The argument here really hinges on the relationship between the parents and the teacher. Where the relationship is one of the consumer or client to those who deliver a service, it is difficult to get across the importance of the parental role in education. However, where the fundamental relation is one of partnership, it is much easier

for parents to see themselves as collaborators in the children's learning in *all* areas of the curriculum. The conclusions in the last chapter deal with the differences between these two ways of construing the relationship between home and school.

Science curriculum evenings can be a very useful way of both involving parents and informing them about how children come to learn science and their potential role in this process. Many schools pick a science topic and construct the evening around this. For example, one school picked the topic of 'Space' and had a massive display in the darkened hall of all the planets and the sun hanging from the ceiling, lit from within, and a rocket which the children had built looming in the corner of the hall. There was a large display of children's work on this topic throughout the school. Another school had a similar evening on the theme of 'growth and development', which was also extremely successful. Through the use of a topic, it is comparatively easy to demonstrate to parents how scientific processes may be developed and the relevant facts and understandings acquired.

HISTORY AND GEOGRAPHY

These subjects lend themselves naturally to two types of collaboration with parents. Firstly, parents – and grandparents – can often be 'providers' here. In approaching a history or geography topic, it is worth considering whether it is possible to include a contribution from one or more of the parents. Clearly, some topics lend themselves to this more easily than others. For example, when studying the two world wars, there may be many points at which the oral history of that time as told by a parent or grandparent will provide an extraordinary source of stimulation for all kinds of work by the children. Not only will such a contribution add depth to their readings of more 'distanced' information in history books, but it may also be the stimulus for their own writing of imagined oral narratives, told as if by people living through these events. However, if the topic is the Tudors and Stuarts, the parental contribution would have to be of a different order. Perhaps parents have or know of artefacts dating from these times, or maybe there are local buildings or areas about which parents possess more personal knowledge.

The 'parent-as-provider' is equally useful in geographical topics, particularly in studying the local area. However, even when children are studying areas far away from the locality, parents can be a valuable source of both experience and knowledge. In a school in the centre of England, children aged 6 and 7 were studying different environments, including that of the sea-coast. A parent who had been a fisherman in Cornwall for many years came in, bringing many of his artefacts and tools and talking about his experiences, good and bad! The children were then much better prepared for the eventual school trip to the coast, and they had an understanding which informed the questions they asked. In terms of studying the locality of the school, parents are often a source not only of information but of expertise. Parents, or other relations living locally, may be able to chart from first-hand experience some of the changes which have taken place and the developments which have been built over the last twenty or thirty years.

In either history or geography, there is really no substitute for these first-hand narrations in terms of their effect on the children's interest and enthusiasm, and the subsequent quality of their work. In addition, including parents in this way conveys some very important messages, both to the children and to the parents themselves, about how we as teachers value the contributions parents can make to the formal, as well as the informal, education of their children. The status-enhancing effects of having parents contribute to the classroom curriculum in this way is immensely valuable in building the partnership mentioned earlier.

The flip side of this coin is the situation where the children are the 'providers' in the context of the home. Children can teach their parents as much as the parents can teach them, in many instances. Children in a London school did a long project stimulated by the diaries of Anne Frank. Some of the information they were acquiring was taken home to parents in the form of information sheets and question-and-answer games devised by the children themselves. This arose because the children themselves felt that it was important to share what they had learned with their parents and the wider community. They felt that many people were not aware of some of the events surrounding Anne Frank's short life, and that they had a role to play in helping to inform their own families.

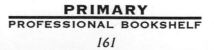

Children acting as 'tutors' in this way is likely, as was mentioned above, to assist the children's learning as much as – if not more than – it assists those they are tutoring. As they go through their questions and answers, making the game a quiz and playing the 'role of the expert', they are making that knowledge *their own* in a very real sense.

ART

It is only at school that most children get to experience many of the media within which we work in art. Clay, silk-screening, printing and even painting on anything other than a small scale are not possible in the majority of homes. Some schools are fortunate enough to have the space and the resources to enable them to invite parents to participate, on specific occasions, in the art project of the moment. A class in a school in one small town was doing a project on the Impressionists. The children were studying a whole variety of paintings by Turner, Monet, van Gogh, Cézanne and others. They had visited a London museum on a day trip and obtained large numbers of postcards and prints. The local library had also supplied them with some books of paintings. On one particular afternoon, the parents were all invited in to share these resources and to help the children to select the ones they were going to emulate in paint themselves, working in pairs. The discussions and the conversations which took place over these pictures, and the ways in which the children were anxious to share their knowledge with all the parents (not just their own), were again of a remarkable quality. This was reflected in the care which the children took with their subsequent painting and the excellence of their results.

Children often draw at home, and the nature and development of these drawings can be a useful starting-point for a more general discussion about the child's progress. In the nursery and the infant school, children's early drawings are linked to their attempts to communicate through writing.[11] It is important that teachers recognise the value of these 'home' offerings, and that we do not convey the idea that all the important things are done at school and all the 'play' is done at home. Learning at home is indeed quintessentially *informal* in character. However, children do often practise skills, especially those required for drawing, at home; and the advances made when they are working in the home context are often important. Most teachers welcome children's drawings, particularly when children feel that they have made a breakthrough or achieved something special. Many children bring drawings or paintings in to 'show teacher'; but it is useful to recognise those where they have worked for a long time to achieve a result, in artistic or technical terms, that they were unable to achieve before.

DESIGN AND TECHNOLOGY

Children also often do a great deal of model building or layout design at home or elsewhere outside the school. Some children in the class of one of the authors spent every single spare moment of a particular term building a space layout for their small *Star Wars* and *Star Trek* plastic figures. They created a whole planet, complete with craters and mountains and a space station. Parts of old cardboard boxes, corrugated card, polystyrene fillings and Lego were all press-ganged into service in the creation of this base. In the end, it was brought (carefully!) into class by the mother of one of the children, and the whole class heard how to make one. The Blue Peter programme a couple of years ago in which they demonstrated how you could make a 'Thunderbirds' island out of cardboard and papier mâché had a similar effect on many groups of small children. Parents swapped stories about the mess caused by having a bowl of flour-and-water glue permanently on the go while the children added to the layers of papier mâché each day! Many of these stories found their way back into classrooms, where the teacher used the papier mâché technique to create other and perhaps more school topic-focused artefacts.

Sometimes children can be encouraged to work with their parents on three-dimensional models for use in the classroom as part of a particular topic. For example, several children in a small village school in Worcestershire had built three-dimensional maps of their route to school. These were used as part of a geography topic on the local environment. A good number of IMPACT schools hold an Easter competition where the aim is to create an egg-mobile. The task is usually set as being to design and make a means of transport for one

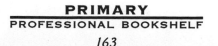

egg (standard size) which is safe, is powered by non-electrical means, and will carry an egg as far as possible. A prize is usually given for the mobile which carries the egg furthest on the day, and also for the most ingenious design!

Setting a task, outlining the parameters and possibly constraining the range of materials which may be used are all familiar aspects of delivering the design and technology curriculum in the classroom. However, it is too infrequently realised that children at home are often engaging in this process, using the means and the resources at their disposal for projects of their own designing. Once parents become aware of the potential educational value of this aspect of the curriculum, they are less inclined to regard their children's activity in this domain as a time-wasting and a messy nuisance, and more likely to see its value and support it. The results can often add a stimulus to the classroom in terms of the children's work in design and technology. A project carried out at home, and even generated by the home (like the space station described earlier), can nevertheless be talked about, discussed and written up in the context of classroom work.

CONCLUSIONS

The ways of involving parents in the wider curriculum are more a question of routine and ongoing good practice than a series of special homework projects. We can summarise the approach outlined in this chapter as 'Be alert!' Teachers need to be alert to two things: the richness and usefulness of the home environment in terms of people and resources, and the amount of help which parents themselves have to offer. A number of practical suggestions have been made:

✦ *Planning: include the parental/community dimension.*
When planning topic work, whether in science, history or geography, think about where parents can contribute. Are there any parents who have a particular expertise? Could the topic draw upon local or personal historical or geographical knowledge? What about the children's wider families – aunts, uncles, grandparents? A contribution from a parent or parents, if planned into the topic at the start, can provide a crucial stimulus at a chosen moment in the children's study.

It is an excellent idea to send home a letter in advance, explaining what the topic is and asking if anyone has any expertise or relevant experiences to share.

◆ *Parents can be 'providers'.*
Parents can be invited into the classroom to give a talk, or share a story told about their own experiences, or use their particular expertise. If possible, this should be planned into the topic in advance. However, on occasion, a teacher will not discover that a parent or a grandparent has some special knowledge or could make a contribution until the topic is actually under way.

◆ *Parents as tutees.*
Children can take home tasks or information to share with their parents. On many occasions the children will be able to explain things to their parents, often things which may be new to the parents themselves. Information can be presented in the form of a quiz which the child carries out with some other members of the family, and the questions should be chosen so that the child knows the answers! It is delightful how often teachers report that parents have themselves been surprised at what they have learned, and at how much their small child knows.

◆ *Welcoming what is done at home.*
Children make things, design things, draw things, read things and write things at home. Many of the skills they utilise are skills which we are keen to have them practise. Recognising that what is done at home can (and often does) form a valuable part of children's education helps to create a situation where the divide between home and school is perceived as one of kind, not one of status, and is seen to be traversable at all points.

◆ *Sending home suitable tasks or activities.*
The SHIPS materials provide a useful and stimulating resource for teachers who would like to build a science aspect into their shared homework programme, alongside the reading, the maths and the writing.

It is also quite easy to construct art or design activities which children can share with someone at home. It is suggested here that these activities should be used to form a part of the regular homework link with parents. If they are also planned into the topic in the same way as was suggested for the parental/community contribution discussed above, then the demands on the teacher may be minimised.

◆ *Informing the parents, via curriculum evenings.*
Curriculum evenings are an obvious and important means by which schools keep parents informed about their approach and the content or subject matter of the curriculum. Building a curriculum evening around a topic can help to make it an interesting and productive way of providing information and demonstrating an educational philosophy. It can also involve the children, both in creating the display and in being there to talk about it. The more the children are involved, the higher (in general) the percentage of parents who will attend.

All of the above suggestions are ways in which a school can convey to its parents the most important message of all. This is that parents are not consumers of an education service. They are partners in an education process. It is to a discussion of the nature of this partnership that we shall turn in our concluding chapter.

REFERENCES

1 See Lave, J. (1986) *Cognition in Practice*.
2 See Light, P. & Butterworth, G. (Eds.) (1992) *Context and Cognition* Harvester/Wheatsheaf.
3 A term used by Martin Hughes *et al* on the ESRC-funded project looking at the transference of mathematical skills. Exeter University, 1994/5.
4 See the proceedings of the Annual Conference of the Centre for Families, Schools, Youth and Communities, chaired by Joyce Epstein and Don Davies in San Francisco, 1995.
5 See Bourdieu, P. & Passeron, J. (1988) *Social Reproduction*;
Bernstein, B. (1988) *Class, Codes and Control*, Vols. 3 & 4;
Brown, A. & Dowling, P. (1990) 'nnnn' in *The Notional not the National Curriculum* Dowling and Noss (Eds.), Falmer Press.

6 Lave, J. & Wenger, E. (1990) *Situated Learning*.

7 See Merttens, R. 'Pedagogy and Intimacy', forthcoming, for a further elaboration of this point.

8 See Chapter 1, also Tizard, B. & Hughes, M. (1984) *Young Children Learning*, Fontana.

9 Goodlad, S. & Hurst, B. (1989) *Peer Tutoring* Kogan Page.

10 Solomon, J. (1991) 'Science Investigations as a School-Home Link' in *Links* 17 (3) 5–8, and

Solomon, J. (1993) *Teaching Science, Technology and Society*, Open University Press.

11 See Chapter 4.

CHAPTER 6

CONCLUSION

I've got some children for whom IMPACT, Shared Writing and the diary is by far the best work they do. One child I can think of gets so much more done at home than in school. And the parents are really pleased with it, you get that back from them all the time... and that's the important bit, it's the dialogue it creates.

Year Four Teacher, North London

In this book, we have tried to offer some signposts which point towards a fruitful collaboration between schools and families, and between teachers, parents and children. We have also tried to offer a range of useful practical strategies for involving parents in a number of curriculum areas, and to ground these practices in a coherent and comprehensible theory which reflects some of the socio-cultural processes of school and family life. In this final chapter, our task will be to return to the rationale for the book and to set out why we think involving parents in the curriculum is a valuable contribution to professional educational practice in general and to raising achievement in particular. We will also reiterate some of the key principles that we think are central to working with parents. Listening to what parents have to say about their own children is one of the most important of these, and reflects the spirit of collaboration that the book is attempting to promote. However, this book has also concerned itself very much with how parental involvement in education can validate the often tacit, spontaneous and 'invisible' educative practices that parents perform by making them more explicit, reflective and 'visible'.

Recently one of the authors was seated behind a father and son on a bus. The boy was about three or four years old, and was kneeling on the seat drawing and writing shapes in the condensation that had formed on the inside of the window. Every few minutes he would turn to his father to show him what he had drawn. Patiently, the boy's father would look up from his newspaper and feign interest. Having used up most of the space available to him, the child began to shift his attention to the label attached to the window, which showed a smoking cigarette on a red background encircled in white with a white band through it.

'What does that say Daddy?'
'No Smoking.'
'That means you can't smoke, doesn't it?'
'Yes, that's right. No smoking on the bus.'

The boy then began putting his fingers over parts of the words and muttering to himself, slowly:

'No... Smoke... King... No... Smoke... King...
That says "No" doesn't it Daddy?' (*pointing to the word 'No'*)
'Yes, that's right.'
'No... Smoke... King... No...Smoke... King...
(*pointing*) That says "king!" That says "king" doesn't it Daddy?'
'Yes it does, yes. Yeh, that's right.' (*surprised*)
'Where does it say "on the bus?"'
'It doesn't say "on the bus" anywhere, but it means no smoking on the bus.'

A number of interesting issues arise out of this short encounter that we do not have time to deal with; but what is striking is the very active role played by the child in developing his own literacy. For a child so young, he is already impressively demonstrating the effective use of a number of learning strategies. While the boy is actively engaged in making sense of the print in his own terms, he is able to engage in the apparently abstract activity of 'breaking up' the words because his father has already contextualised them in meaning for him. The apparent lack of support he gets from his father is therefore misleading. Though his father is peripheral to the activity (by his reading of a newspaper), he responds to his son at crucial points which are contingent upon the boy's needs.

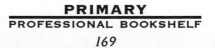

An observation of a similar nature took place on a London Underground train. Once again it involved a father, and this time two children: a girl of about six or seven and a boy of about four. The children and father all had 'cockney' accents and were wearing worn clothing. My interest in this family was strong, because of the high level of conversational engagement between the three participants, which after some time became quite compelling.

We pick up the conversation some time after they have boarded the train:

Girl: One... two... three... four... five... six... seven... eight to Covent Garden.

Boy: Where's Convent Garden?

Father: Covent Garden. Cov...ent Garden... see it.

    (*pointing to the station sign through the train window*)

G: There it is. Jason.

    (*pointing to the Underground Line map above their heads*)

B: Is the train having a rest?

F: That's right.

G: Daddy, where are we going?

F: South Kensington. Count how many we have to go.

    (*For some minutes the girl is absorbed in counting the stations on the overhead map. Then she looks at the sign on the station where the train has stopped.*)

G: Next is Leicester Square.

F: That's right.

B: Where's Mister Square?

F: Leicester Square.

G: Look, Jason, I'll show you.

    (*sitting up on the seat and looking for it*)

F: How many to go?

G: One... two... three... four... Four.

F: No, that's to Knightsbridge. We want the one after that.

As the train rocks from side to side, the boy sways from side to side but exaggerates the motion of the train. The father mirrors his behaviour.

He then holds up both hands with the palms facing each other, and attempts to show by the use of his hands the rocking motion of the train cushioned by suspension. He gives a verbal explanation which is inaudible because of the train noise.

> G: Is that where we're going?
> F: No, that's Knightsbridge.
> B: Night... bridge...
> F: (*speaking to the girl*) The one after Hyde Park Corner.
> Two after Green Park. Three after Piccadilly Circus.
> B: Where's the night bridge?
>   (*The girl begins counting again*)
> F: The one Emma's got her finger on now.

Clearly, the conceptualisation of numeracy and that of literacy here are not only deeply interrelated, but are also deeply embedded in the context. To attempt to disentangle one from the other would also have the effect of diminishing the analysis. The same is true of analysing the interactive roles of the participants. To focus on one and ignore the others would be to lose the richness of the interaction taken as a whole. Indeed, in terms of the socio-historical methods of enquiry that were pioneered by Vygotsky,[1] the validity of the whole method is completely undermined unless we view individuals in their social and cultural contexts. More will be said about this later.

Perhaps the most obvious thing to say is that the parent-father is clearly in the role of a teacher-instructor – and by this account, quite a good one at that. He engages in *teaching* here, not on the basis of any explicit curriculum (at least not one which is drawn from an abstract and distant authority), but on the basis of a curriculum which is immediate to the functional, personal and interest needs of his children at that moment. His teaching is also contingent upon what he perceives to be the interest needs of his children expressed by the questions they are asking. In other words, he does not simply set an agenda: he also responds to the one they construct. The conversation is spontaneous and relaxed; and though no special resources are available, he enlists the resources and media of the immediate environment effortlessly and to good effect. Though there is a high adult-child ratio, he is also managing the learning of a 'vertical age group', and is able to draw on the expertise of the older daughter to help with the collaborative learning of the younger son. The context also allows for continuous, uninterrupted, extended conversation where any assessment of the children is both informal and formative.

To be specific, in attempting to make sense of the unfamiliar utterance 'Covent Garden' the boy converts it into one with which he is presumably more familiar: 'Convent Garden'. The matter-of-fact correction from the father comes with the skilful use of some additional pedagogical tools: first the father re-articulates the utterance 'Cov... ent Garden'; then he directs the boy's attention to the words on the station sign, first by saying 'See it' and then by pointing to the words themselves. Unconcerned that he may not be making sense, the boy again 'tries out' the sense of the unfamiliar utterances 'Mister Square' and 'night bridge' on his father, apparently confident that his father will patiently help him to make sense of whatever does not make sense to him at that moment. Duly, he does so; the boy asks 'Where's Mister Square?' and his father emphasises and articulates the phonemes in 'Leicester Square'. Elsewhere, the father can be seen to set tasks for his daughter, who is older and can therefore be judged more able to tackle these tasks. Once again, the father is making tacit decisions based on the principle that what he needs to feed in or teach as a father-teacher is contingent upon what the child needs to know in order to maintain an interest and operate functionally in the context. In the parent's terms, that means keeping children from getting bored on a train journey.

So even in this short period of time (the whole sequence lasted only about ten minutes), the father has demonstrated an impressive range of teaching skills which include **instructing** (One after Hyde Park Corner... two after Green Park... three after Piccadilly Circus); **directing attention** (Cov... ent Garden. See it. (pointing)); **narrating an explanation** (explaining the motion of the suspension of the train [though unheard]); **modelling** (using his hands to show the motion of suspension of the train); **correcting** (No, that's Knightsbridge). More than that, when one compares the nature and character of the learning that took place in this example with the nature and character of the learning that takes place in

classrooms, we should be forced to reflect on and review any assumptions we make about parents 'doing more harm than good' when teaching their children. This interaction was not constrained (as we have said) by an imposed curriculum, nor did it seem to require much planning or effort on the part of the participants. The interaction was neither timetabled nor of a fixed duration, nor contrived for the purpose of teaching. Nor was it formally tested, assessed or dependent on special equipment or resources. It involved a high adult-child ratio and drew on the expertise of both the adult as instructor and the more able peer/sibling in an interactive, collaborative mode of teaching and learning.

In both these cases, the parent-fathers are not only helping their children to read, write or count, but are playing out a complex cultural activity through which children can achieve higher levels of social and cognitive functioning. For Vygotsky, the formation of such functioning (indeed of consciousness itself) takes place on two levels: first, on the social plane by virtue of social interaction and activity; and second, on the individual plane as internalised cognition.

> Every function in the cultural development of the child appears on the stage twice, on two planes. First, on the social plane, and then on the psychological; first, between people, and then, inside the child.[2]

In other words, a concept, a skill or a knowledge that we acquire or appropriate by virtue of activity in a social context becomes part of our own internalised, individual functioning. The process by which this acquisition takes place is through the cultural use of the tools of language – in this case, the signs and symbols that were enlisted to mediate learning from the parent to the child:

> first, collective activity, then culture, the (...) sign or symbol, and finally individual consciousness.[3]

so when the boy asks 'Where's Convent Garden?' he initiates the potential for activity between himself and his father. His father responds by engaging him in what Vygotsky calls cultural activity – in other words, using the tools of our psychological functioning (language: signs and symbols) to mediate learning to him:

> 'Covent Garden. Cov...ent Garden... see it.' (*pointing to the station sign through the train window*)
> 'There it is, Jason,' says his sister (*pointing to the station on the Underground Line map*), who has already reached the stage of having internalised the sign and joins in the mediating collaboration.

The authentic nature and quality of the collaboration here is underlined by the way each child brings a personal contribution at his or her own level. This is not a one-sided activity of one adult with one child, but an interaction of mutual assistance where the adult and the children are of help to each other.[4] The children are being helped by their father (and each other) to learn about signs, symbols, language, counting, sequences, train suspension, journeys and whatever else. The parent-father is being helped by the children to use the possibilities of the social interaction and to direct and regulate their learning within this specific social context. Vygotsky wrote the following as long ago as 1926:

> A psychological law states: before you want to involve the child in some kind of activity, interest the child in it, being concerned to make sure that the child is ready for this activity, that all the child's strengths needed for it are exerted, that the child will act for him/herself, and that for the teacher remains only the task of guiding and directing the child's activity.[5]

What is so revolutionary about Vygotsky's method for the psychology of his time, and what still reverberates through educational practice in the late twentieth century, is the notion that the educative process is active in three ways. Not only are the teacher (or parent) and the learner (or child) active agents in the process, but the context which they have constructed is also active – not least because it is the site within which the signs, symbols and artefacts of our culture and history are deeply embedded. Teachers and learners re-create culture by mediating these signs, symbols and artefacts through meaning-making activities such as talking, writing, reading, solving maths problems, investigating scientific phenomena or whatever else might happen in school. Parents and their children also do it by making a meal together, going shopping or talking about the stations on a London Underground journey. This is what Vygotsky sees as the dialectical process of language interaction – that is, how the human need to learn creates socially collaborative but also socially conflicting conditions, out of which emerges something new and fruitful.

Interactions like those described above go on every day in families, yet they are largely tacit in that parents themselves may not recognise the pedagogical aspects of the incidents. Also, they are almost completely spontaneous in that they are not incited from external sources such as a syllabus or curriculum. Because they are both tacit and spontaneous, and because they occur in contexts quite separate from the school and classroom, in many ways they can be said to be 'invisible' as pedagogic practices (though not necessarily as social practices). We would want to emphasise that we are not using the term 'visible' in the way that Basil Bernstein has used it. Rather, the notion of visibility we use here is drawn from Jean Lave and Etienne Wenger's account of analysing apprenticeship models of learning.[6] What is helpful about the Lave and Wenger account is that they use the metaphor of a window being created by the teacher to make visible the world outside.

In school contexts, the reverse is the case. While many socialising practices remain implicit, pedagogic practices are quite explicit and are the subject of our planning diaries, school policies, National Curriculum documents, staff meetings and in-service courses. Though many of us may recall some of our best teaching being done spontaneously, our professional training has geared us to plan and prepare in quite systematic and scientific ways. What we do is required to be visible, not least because this is one of the ways we are made accountable as professionals.

It may help to provide a concrete example of this 'rendering visible' process. Parents, particularly mothers, routinely sort the washing into different piles. The IMPACT maths pack contains a 'sorting' activity where the parent and the child sort the washing together, discuss the various criteria and categories, and count how many items are in each pile. This is commonly a successful and popular activity. Thereafter, the parent is aware not only of the pragmatic aspects of this social practice, but also of its pedagogic aspects. These pedagogic aspects have been 'rendered visible' by the IMPACT task, and the parent may choose to focus on, or develop further, these aspects of the job in hand.

We argue that many school-initiated shared home-based tasks have this function of rendering visible the pedagogic aspects of social practices. Parents may choose to ignore these aspects – once the actual homework is over – or they may decide to highlight them, but now they have a choice.

These invisible and visible pedagogies are not so separate that they do not influence each other. Clearly, the overwhelming evidence of research confirms that what parents do with their children outside school can have enormous influence on pupil achievement. What is less certain is whether the social and pedagogic practices of 'the family' influence schools unless the school is aware of and open to such influences. The relationship of the 'spontaneous' to the 'scientific' is one that Vygotsky has focused on closely in the development of his theory of teaching and learning.[7] He describes a model of conceptual development in which spontaneous and scientific concepts have a dynamic and structuring relationship to each other. Spontaneous concepts are those developed by a child's own mental activity, whereas 'scientific' concepts are developed with the assistance of expert knowledge offered through adult instruction. Spontaneous concepts evolve (metaphorically speaking) 'upwards', to become more systematic as they engage with the 'scientific' models of expertise provided by teachers (or more able peers). Scientific concepts, on the other hand, evolve 'downwards' and become integrated into a child's concrete and spontaneous operations. In other words, as we interact socially with more expert adults or peers, we acquire and appropriate concepts and skills into our own body of knowledge. This process, a dynamic and dialectical one (in Vygotsky's view), is the

constant condition of the teacher-learner relationship. The teacher becomes a learner by virtue of reflecting on her own explicitly mediated teaching. The learner becomes a teacher by virtue of mediating to others what he has learned in order to know it through reflection. In terms of teachers working with parents, parents gain because they can feel a satisfaction from a heightened sense of their parenting skills. Teachers gain because they are reflecting, and thereby understanding better what they do.

Our rationale for involving parents in the curriculum is therefore informed by Vygotsky's model of conceptual development. In attempting to theorise the specifically pedagogic relationship between school and home, it may be helpful to invoke the scientific/spontaneous dichotomy. As we have indicated already, 'scientific' in this context is not to be taken literally: it means the systematic and expert assistance afforded by teachers to learners. But learners, of course, are not passive recipients of knowledge; and as the term 'spontaneous' suggests, they are active and constructive both of their own knowledge and of the way they are being taught by their teacher. The 'scientific' teacher and the 'spontaneous' learner are therefore reflexive and responsive to each other.

The table shown in Figure 1 is thus not to be interpreted in terms of a dichotomous division, but rather a situation where the contexts, agents and pedagogies of learning are in a dynamic and dialectical relationship with each other.

There are two important points to remember in discussing this table. The first is that the categories are not related to the headings 'Scientific' and 'Spontaneous' in any literal, direct way. We are using these categories as analogies to Vygotsky's categories. The second point is that the scientific and the spontaneous categories are not related to each other in any hierarchical way, in spite of Vygotsky's 'upward' and 'downward' metaphor. Their relationship is characterised much more by a view of them as being dynamically and reciprocally structured and restructured. The scientific constantly *informs* the spontaneous. The spontaneous constantly *reforms* the scientific.

We are not advocating or presuming that the school has a role in structuring the family practices of the home, even those which have a pedagogic aspect. However, the school can have a legitimate and

Figure 1	'Scientific'	'Spontaneous'
Contexts	schools	homes
Agents	teachers parents children teachers professionals	pupils children children parents laity
Pedagogies	school explicit visible	home tacit invisible

fruitful role in enabling parents to develop a conscious reflection of certain family practices, particularly in ways that might provide for more critical engagement in such practices. In previous chapters we have described how some activities initiated from school fulfil this role.

It is an important part of the emphasis of this book to relate this idea to the nature of the partnership between teachers and parents. Though in some important respects the interests of teachers and parents are different, collaboration which arises out of the interests of the child is the basis on which partnerships can be built. Teachers can become better teachers in this way, because collaboration with parents can inform them in great detail about (and with great insight into) the child, of whom the parent has expert knowledge. This information helps teachers to reflect and even to reform their practice. Parents can collaborate with teachers, whose professional knowledge about teaching and learning can inform and enhance pedagogic aspects of family life. By doing so, they help make visible what parents do – so that it means more to themselves, to their children and to others.

THE COLLABORATIVE PARTNERSHIP APPROACH

We do not wish to suggest that we should always be viewing parental involvement from the self-interested standpoint of schools and teachers. We want to develop a view of parental involvement which is based on active collaboration and partnership and which takes account of the experiences of parents and families for their own value. We want to promote a view which values the knowledge, experience and resources that parents possess and recognises the contribution they can make. We want to suggest that schools should see their relationship to parents as that of co-participants in the education of their children, where the accent is on developing a dialogue in which parents are seen to have rights as well as obligations and responsibilities.

In recent years, the political climate and the introduction of the Parents' Charter have created a different kind of perception: one dominated by a political rhetoric which is often confusing and unhelpful and which attempts to position parents as consumers in relation to the school as a provider, apparently driven by competitive market forces. Recent legislative changes have radically repositioned schools and parents, and the shift in the balance and exercise of power has inevitably created some tension and even conflict.

Although schools and families are very different things, and at times their concerns may seem at odds, they do share some important common values and interests; and it is the pursuit of these common interests that this book has tried to focus on positively. While we recognise the potential political advantage in conceptualising the issues in terms of free market rhetoric,[8] we prefer to emphasise that participative aspect of the consumer-provider relationship which 'conceives consumers as exercising influence through dialogue and shared decision-making'.[9]

The work of John Bastiani[10] has been influential in developing parental involvement in this country. His emphasis outlines six main strands in the development of a collaborative partnership approach towards education. The account below elaborates further on some of these points.

SUPPORTING PARENTS

Much work on family literacy[11], both here and in the United States, points to the conclusion that unless families are supported with their own literacy practices (perhaps through the setting up of a family literacy programme) then much effort will be wasted. Other material support is needed, such as offering the facilities of the school to set up a parent and toddler group or the use of a Parents' Room to host activities from which parents can develop skills and gain confidence (see Chapter 1 for details). Using the expertise of parents in the classroom to cook, translate or interpret, to run a sports team or handicraft group, or to demonstrate a skill or hobby, is an important way of supporting the social and cultural background of the parent community.

LISTENING TO PARENTS

As we have indicated, parents are important providers of information. Through the regular use of home-school diaries (such as those used for IMPACT) or through parent conferences (such as those used in connection with the Primary Learning Record),[12] a forum for listening to the views of parents is established. Perhaps more important is the dialogue that this forum can create. Listening to parents' accounts of family life can yield an enormous amount of valuable information for teachers, which can have a direct influence on their practice. Parents are 'experts' on their own children; they observe what their children enjoy doing and are good at outside the narrow context of school life.

DEVELOPING A DIALOGUE WITH PARENTS

Teachers of young children know the importance of establishing and developing an ongoing dialogue with parents if the children are to feel confident and thrive in the early years of their education. Responding to information through home-school diaries has become a crucial mechanism by which the success and usefulness of home-school liaison is judged in many schools. Research on IMPACT[13] and the Shared Writing Project has shown that many teachers value the dialogue created by the diary more than the direct pedagogical benefits of the activities that accompany them. Building times to meet regularly with parents into the calendar of the school year is one way that many schools have responded to innovations in this area. The work of the Centre for Language in Primary Education in devising and developing the Primary Language Record and the Primary Learning Record has been a major contribution to developing and improving a dialogue with parents focused on parental perceptions and accounts of their children's learning.

INFORMING PARENTS

Informing parents about teaching methods, approaches and curriculum developments through workshop evenings or open classroom days has now become a well-established and successful practice around the country. Some schools use notice-boards imaginatively, with colourful displays attracting parents to notices which are dedicated to their child's class or year group. Some schools have notice-boards for parents which are maintained by them. One school we visit in North London has a regular newsletter which informs parents of the class topics and projects for the coming term and invites them to share their interests, stories, artefacts or whatever.

INVOLVING PARENTS IN THE LIFE
AND WORK OF THE SCHOOL

Many schools draw on important human resources by encouraging parents to be helpers on school outings, raise funds for equipment purchase or organise events such as fairs and socials. A school in High Wycombe has a thriving 'Parents as Teachers Group' with a series of well-planned and resourced practical workshops, discussion groups and meetings in a dedicated parents' room. The group is serviced by regular newsletters, and produces brochures and school magazines. Another school we have worked with has made particular efforts to involve parents in sports and games activities, and in helping to run sports and athletics clubs.

INVOLVING PARENTS IN THEIR
OWN CHILDREN'S LEARNING

Parents are perhaps most keen to help with their own children's learning, and this can be done in school or at home through shared or paired reading, writing or maths activities (as well as such experiences

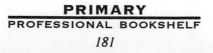

as attending assemblies given by a child's class). One of the authors used to end the school day by asking the children what they had done during the day that they would like to tell their parents about when they got home. Parents were similarly encouraged to ask their children. This is a simple but very effective way to mediate information about what is happening in school and to help develop a dialogue between child and parent.

Much of the recent research on school improvement referred to by Coleman and Collinge[14] suggests that the extent to which pupils and parents feel the teachers at their school to be 'collaborative' (that is to say, they feel they can influence what goes on in the school) determines how positive the school climate will be. Their evidence suggests that this depends very largely on the class teacher and not the headteacher, which is heartening for individual teachers trying to establish collaborative parental involvement ventures without the enthusiasm of other, more senior colleagues. Even if the school is perceived by parents as 'bad', the collaborative attitude of the teacher is a crucial factor which (particularly at primary level) can override the choice of school. Indeed, parents of primary-age children are much more interested in the 'choice' of their child's class teacher, a matter on which they rarely have any influence at all.

Coleman and Collinge refer to measures of school improvement which show that effective collaboration between teachers, parents and children is five times more significant than all other factors put together. The other factors include indicators such as class size and resources. They also found that the communicative relationship between the parents and the school is highly influential on pupil-teacher relationships and pupil-parent satisfaction. This is supported by research on projects such as IMPACT which strongly emphasise the role of the diary as the crucial mechanism for building a dialogue between home and school. What is important to parents, according to Coleman and Collinge, is that the school welcomes parental involvement (even if this is restricted to an annual 'Meet the Teacher' night) and that teachers are perceived to have a collaborative attitude.

Many teachers will know from experience that the most effective way of attracting parents to curriculum evenings or events is to make personal approaches. While this targets only a section of the parent body, it is an effective strategy both for advertising an event and for building up personal relationships and channels of effective communication. Many people judge an institution by the way it communicates. Although clear and direct (but informal and accessible) letters, brochures and posters are important for those parents with whom personal contact is difficult, schools should remember that the experience of being communicated with can determine attitudes. When trains are cancelled, waiting passengers often get more angry about lack of communication than they do about the cancelled train.

Parents also value a variety of forms of communication. If the same photocopied typewritten format with a reply slip at the bottom is the invariable form of the letter home, it will probably have a similar impact to the daily junk mail and may well receive the same treatment. Some parents will always prefer personal contact, especially if their own literacy is poor – though of course, it is not always possible to speak to individuals at length; it may be a more efficient use of teacher time to speak to parents in small groups or to the parent body as a whole.

Teachers need to be aware that the use of professional jargon can be quite confusing and alienating to parents, and that its use as a weapon to bamboozle inquisitive parents is as unwise as it is unprofessional. Roger Hancock advises that 'constructive communication is a shared responsibility and both teachers and parents need to make an effort'.[15] Sometimes parents will feel unwelcome even when teachers have felt they have been reassuring and communicative. Some parents have reported[16] that they were encouraged to 'get in touch with the school if they or their children had any particular problems'. As they had no particular *problems*, they felt unsure about whether it was appropriate to approach the school.

Inviting parental involvement can open up large resources of knowledge, skills and expertise that teachers lack; but it also involves enormous risks for the social dynamics of the school. Parental involvement can result in parents' improved understanding and more positive views of what the school is trying to do. It may result in support for such issues as staffing levels, the condition and repair of buildings and the supply of equipment and resources.

The diverse nature of class, gender, race and culture is a great source of wealth to a school, but it can also be a source of confused perceptions. One voluntary-aided Church of England school we have worked with

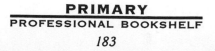

noticed that although the school served a socially and culturally mixed community, the Asian parents were proportionately less involved in school activities than other parents. Eventually staff realised that school events, even non-religious ones, almost always coincided with religious holidays of the Christian calendar. When the school began to vary the calendar of social events, they found a change in participation rates.

Parents are also aware of how their own modelling of behaviours and skills, such as reading, writing, cooking, handicrafts and mechanics, can be reflected in the way their children learn. Children will also learn much from other members of the family, and information on how brothers, sisters, grandparents and others assist, challenge, support or inhibit the learning of a child is valuable to teachers. Parents are very skilled in observing, evaluating and assessing their children's behaviour and then responding and intervening in learning opportunities.[17] The responsive and contingent nature of teaching and learning at home can make them an important source of insight for assessing the needs, including the special needs, of children in the context of school.

Every staffroom has its apocryphal stories of 'pushy middle-class parents' who are constantly 'pressurising' teachers and children. Then there are those parents who are 'totally unsupportive' and who are 'the ones you most want to see but never do'. Though we can identify with such sympathies, we would urge our readers not to generalise about parents any more than they would about teachers. Any group of parents is diverse and heterogeneous, and professional teachers should view the inclusion of 'reluctant' parents as a positive challenge to their professional credibility rather than an excuse for inaction and low expectation. Indeed, teachers who view parents as participants in the education of their children have a privileged perspective. When teachers develop strategies that utilise the specialist knowledge of the parent in collaboration with the professional knowledge of the teacher, drawing on the social (and pedagogic) practices of the home to inform the pedagogic (and social) practices of the school, then the complementary roles of teacher and parent are greatly enhanced and the interests of children are enormously advanced. The work of Coleman and Collinge (referred to earlier) emphasises strongly that parent involvement in their children's learning is not the 'icing on the cake', but is actually central to school improvement and pupil achievement.

We have often referred to writers and thinkers who have contributed to socio-cultural and socio-historical conceptions of knowledge in order to inform our theoretical framework for the practical suggestions we have offered in this book. Mikhail Bakhtin, a Russian literary critic writing largely before the Second World War, reminds us of the essentially dialogic nature of human communication. He describes how, as we speak or think about what we say, we inevitably have to take into account the 'voices' of others:

> Every utterance must be regarded as primarily a response to preceding utterances of a given sphere... Each utterance refutes, affirms, supplements and relies upon the others, presupposes them to be known and somehow takes them into account...[18]

There are many 'voices' that construct us in our personal and professional lives. What we have argued in this book is that one of the 'voices' which acts to structure both pedagogical and professional practices should be that of the parents themselves. We must recognise, value and utilise the voices of parents as necessary and legtimate contributions to the dialogue which constitutes education. What this dialogue then embodies is the collaborative partnership of teachers, parents and their children.

REFERENCES

1 See Vygotsky's *Thought and Language* (1986) and *Mind in Society* (1978) – sometimes difficult, but always worth it.

2 Vygotsky, L.S. (1978) *Mind in Society*, p 128.

3 Vygotsky in Davydov, V.V. (1995), p 16.

4 Davydov (1995), p 17.

5 Vygotsky (1926) in Davydov (1995), p 17.

6 See Lave, J. and Wenger, E. (1991), especially Chapter 4.

7 See Vygotsky (1986), especially Chapters 5 and 6.

8 See Woods, P. (1993) for an interesting discussion on parents as consumer citizens.

9 Woods, P. (1993), p 16.

10 See Bastiani, J. *et al* (1988).

11 See Taylor, D. and Dorsey-Gaines, C. (1988).

12 See their publications *The Primary Language Record* (1988) and *Guide to the Primary Learning Record* (1990).

13 See Merttens, R. and Vass, R. (1990 & 1993).

14 Coleman, P. and Collinge, J. (1995) 'The Cycle of Effects: School Climate and Parent and Student Integration': a paper delivered at the IMPACT Annual Conference held at the University of North London, June 30th–July 1st 1995.

15 See Roger Hancock's article in *Language Matters* 1993/4, No. 3, p 16.

16 See Bastiani, J. *et al* (1988), p 81.

17 See Bastiani, J. *et al* (1988), p 96.

18 Bakhtin, M. quoted in Shotter, J. (1993).

BIBLIOGRAPHY

ALBSU The Basic Skills Unit (1995) *Developing Family Literacy*, ALBSU.

Atkin, J., Bastiani, J. with Goode, J. (1988) *Listening to Parents: An Approach to the Improvement of Home-School Relations*, Croom Helm.

Austin, J. (1962) *How to do things with words*, Oxford University Press.

Barrs, M., Ellis, S., Hester, H. and Thomas, A. (1988) *The Primary Language Record: Handbook for Teachers*, ILEA.

Barrs, M. and Thomas, A. (Eds.) (1991)*The Reading Book*, CLPE.

Barton, D. (1994) *Literacy: An Introduction to the Ecology of Written Language*, Blackwell.

Bastiani, J. (1989) *Working with Parents: a whole school approach*, NFER-Nelson.

Browne, A. (1993) *Helping Children to Write*, Paul Chapman Publishing.

Bruner, J. (1983) *Child's Talk: Learning to Use Language*, Oxford University Press.

Buckingham, D. (1993) *Children Talking Television: The Making of Television Literacy*, Falmer Press.

Calkins, L. M. (1994) *The Art of Teaching Writing* (New Edition), Heinemann.

Centre for Language in Primary Education (1990) *Shared Reading, Shared Writing*, CLPE.

Clay, M. (1975) *What Did I Write?*, Heinemann.

Davis, C. and Stubbs, R. (1988) *Shared Reading in Practice*, Open University Press.

Davydov, V.V. (1995) 'The Influence of L. S. Vygotsky on Education Theory, Research and Practice', in *Educational Researcher*, Vol. 24, No. 3, pp 12–21.

Dentith, S. (1995) *Bakhtinian thought: an introductory reader*, Routledge.

Department of Education and Science (DES) (1990) *The Teaching and Learning of Reading in Primary Schools*, HMSO.

Dombey, H. and Meek Spencer, M. (Eds.) (1994) *First Steps Together: Home-School Early Literacy in European Contexts*, Trentham Books.

Donaldson, M. (1978) *Children's Minds*, Fontana.

Ferreiro, E. and Teberovsky, A. (1979) *Literacy Before Schooling*, Heinemann.

Fish, S. (1980) *Is there a text in this class? The Authority of Interpretive Communities*, Harvard University Press.

Frière, P. (1972) *Pedagogy of the Oppressed*, Pelican.

Glatteor, R. and Woods, P. (1992) *Parental Choice and School Decision-Making: Operating in a Market-like Environment* Commonwealth Council for Educational Administration, University of Hong Kong.

Goody, J. (1981) *The Interface Between the Written and the Oral*, Cambridge University Press.

Graves, D. (1983) *Writing: Teachers and Children at Work*, Heinemann.

Griffiths, A. and Hamilton, D. (1984) *Parent, Teacher, Child: Working Together in Children's Learning*, Methuen.

Grotberg, E. 'The Parental Role in Education and Child Development', in

Dioxedes, S. (Ed.) *(1979) The Child and the World of Tomorrow*, Pergamon Press.

Halliday, M. (1975) *Learning How To Mean*, Elsevier (New York).
Hamilton, M., Barton, D. and Ivanic, R. (Eds.) (1994) *Worlds of Literacy*, Multilingual Matters.
Hannon, P. and Jackson, A. (1987) *The Bellfield Reading Project Final Report*, National Children's Bureau.
Hannon, P. (1995) *Literacy, Home and School: Research and Practice in Teaching Literacy with Parents*, Falmer Press.
Heath, S. B. (1982) 'What no bedtime story means: Narrative skills at home and at school', in *Language in Society*, No.11, pp 49-76.
Heath, S. B. (1983) *Ways with Words: Language, Life, and Work in Communities and Classrooms*, Cambridge University Press.
Hodge, B. and Tripp, D. (1986) *Children and Television: A Semiotic Approach*, Blackwell.
Holquist, M. (1990) *Dialogism: Bakhtin and his World*, Routledge New Accents.
Hughes, M. (1986) *Children and Number*, Blackwell.
Hughes, M., Wikeley, F. and Nash, T. (1994) *Parents and their Children's Schools*, Blackwell.
Ivanic, R. and Hamilton, M. (1989) 'Literacy Beyond Schooling', in Wray, D. (ed.) (1989) *Emerging Partnerships in Language and Literacy*, Multilingual Matters.
Kimberley, K., Meek, M. and Miller, J. (1992) *New Readings: Contributions to an understanding of literacy*, A & C Black.
Kress, G. (1994) *Learning to Write* (Second Edition), Routledge.
Kristeva, J. (1989) *Language, the Unknown*, Columbia University Press.
Language Matters Journal (1993/4) No 3., Parents and Teachers Centre for Language in Primary Education.
Lave, J. (1986) *Cognition in Practice*, Harvard University Press.
Lave, J. and Wenger, E. (1991) *Situated Learning: Legitimate peripheral participation*, Cambridge University Press.
Meek, M. and Mills, C. (Eds.) (1988) *Language and Literacy in the Primary School*, Falmer Press.
Merttens, R. (1994) 'The IMPACT Project in Haringey: Raising Standards in Inner City Schools'. Report to the Department For Education.
Merttens, R. (forthcoming) *Pedagogy and Intimacy*.
Merttens, R., Mayers, D., Brown, A. and Vass, J. (1993) *Ruling the Margins: Problematising Parental Involvement*, University of North London Press.
Merttens, R., Newland, A. and Webb, S. (forthcoming) *The Shared Writing Project Teaching Materials*, Scholastic.
Merttens, R. and Newland, A. (1995) 'IMPACT' at AERA 1995, University of North London Press.
Merttens, R. and Vass, J. (1990) *Sharing Maths Cultures*, Falmer Press.
Merttens, R. and Vass, J. (1993) *Partnerships in Maths: Parents and Schools*, Falmer Press.
Merttens, R. and Woods, P. (1994) 'IMPACT' at AERA 1994, University of North London.

Messenger Davies, M. (1989) *Television is Good for your Kids*, Hilary Shipman.

Minns, H. (1990) *Read it to me now!*, Virago.

Moll, L. C. (Ed.) (1990)*Vygotsky and Education: Instructional Implications and Applications of Sociohistorical Psychology*, Cambridge University Press.

National Writing Project, The (1990) 'Writing Partnerships 1: Home, School and Community', Nelson/SCDC.

Ong, W. (1982) *Orality and Literacy: The Technologising of the Word*, Routledge.

Pierce, C. S. (1931) 'Collected Papers', Hartshorne and Weiss (Eds.), Harvard University Press.

Rosen, M. (1989) *Did I Hear You Write?*, André Deutsch.

de Saussure, F. (1922) *Course in General Linguistics*, Payot.

Soloman, J. (1993) *Teaching Science, Technology and Society*, Open University Press.

Smith, F. (1982) *Writing and the Writer*, Heinemann.

Stubbs, M. (1980) *Language and Literacy: The Sociolinguistics of Reading and Writing*, Routledge.

Stubbs, M. (1986) *Educational Linguistics*, Blackwell.

Taverner, D. (1990) *Reading Within and Beyond the Classroom*, Open University Press.

Taylor, D. and Dorsey-Gaines, C. (1988) *Growing Up Literate*, Heinemann.

Temple, C., Nathan, G. and Burris, N. (1982) *The Beginnings of Writing*, Allyn & Bacon. (Second Edition 1988.)

Tizard, B. and Hughes, M. (1984) *Young Children Learning*, Fontana.

Tizard, J., Schofield, W.N. and Hewison, J. (1982) 'Collaboration between teachers and parents in assisting children's reading', in *British Journal of Educational Psychology*, 52, pp 1-15.

Tizard, B., Blatchford, P., Burke, J., Faruhar, C. and Plewis, I. (1988) *Young Children at School in the Inner City*, Lawrence Erlbaum Associates.

Topping, K. and Wolfendale, S. (Eds.) (1985) *Parental Involvement in Children's Learning*, Croom Helm.

Vygotsky, L.S. (1978) *Mind in Society: The Development of Higher Psychological Processes*, Harvard University Press.

Walberg, H.J. and Marjoribanks, K. (1976) 'Family Environment and Cognitive Development', in *Review of Educational Research 46*, pp 527-551, National Commission on Education, Paul Hamlyn Foundation.

Waterland, L. (1988) *Read with Me: an apprenticeship approach to reading*, The Thimble Press.

Willes, M. (1983) *Children into Pupils*, Routledge & Kegan Paul.

Wells, G. (1986) *The Meaning Makers: children learning language and using language to learn*, Hodder & Stoughton.

Wood, D. (1988) *How Children Think and Learn*, Blackwell.

Woods, P. (1993) 'Parents as Consumer-Citizens', in Merttens, R., Mayers, D., Brown, A. and Vass, J. *Ruling the Margins: Problematising Parental Involvement*, University of North London Press.

INDEX